FINDING THE LIGHT
THROUGH THE DARKNESS

Get wisdom, get understanding;
do not forget my words or turn away from them.
Do not forsake wisdom, and she will protect you;
love her, and she will watch over you.
The beginning of wisdom is this: Get wisdom.
Though it cost all you have, get understanding.
Cherish her, and she will exalt you;
embrace her, and she will honor you.
She will give you a garland to grace your head
and present you with a glorious crown.

—Proverbs 4:5-9

Kabbalah Centre Publishing is a registered DBA of Kabbalah Centre International, Inc.

For further information:

The Kabbalah Centre
1062 S. Robertson Blvd., Los Angeles, CA 90035
155 E. 48th St., New York, NY 10017

1.800.Kabbalah www.kabbalah.com

Printed in USA, March 2016

ISBN: 978-1-952895-54-8

Front cover image ©Johnér/Offset.com
Design: HL Design (Hyun Min Lee) www.hldesignco.com

FINDING THE LIGHT THROUGH THE DARKNESS

Inspirational lessons rooted in the Bible and the Zohar

KABBALAH
CENTRE
PUBLISHING

KAREN BERG

DEDICATION

Rav,

What can I say about how much you mean to me, all that we have been through together and all that I have learned from you?

When we started on our journey we were just the four of us— you and I, and my two girls. We had $4000 to our name. You wanted us to live in Israel. I did not because I did not know the language. We had no family there. People were against us. But somehow you helped me to see why you wanted us to be there. Slowly, in your way, you touched the heart of one person at a time, just as you had touched mine. One by one, sharing your passion for this wisdom and path.

Today, I look around, and there are so many Kabbalah Centres across the world and thousands of people to whom I am so grateful to be of service. Who would have thought? And I can honestly say that none of it would have happened without your persistence and certainty, constantly pushing us forward. You would not turn aside when you knew that it was the right thing to do.

This was not naturally my way. I was like the wind going in seven different directions. But you taught me the most important lesson of my life: When you know you are doing the right thing, let nothing stop you. Persist until you see it through.

This is your gift to me and to everyone you touch—the ability to see the end point, and to go until you reach it.

I had searched so many spiritual paths, but I never found my way until I found you.

So many lifetimes I waited to be together in this one. It was worth the wait.

I love you so very much and am grateful for the certainty and strength you have given and continue to give to me and to the world.

—Karen

PREFACE

I have always felt a calling for spiritual work. Even before I met the Rav, I was immersed in spirituality. Though, it was only after we met that I realized we could create something that would help people and generate change in this world. I believe we came together for that purpose. And so I began to take all the wisdom the Rav received from his world and the knowledge I gained, and to marry the two.

That is how we started The Kabbalah Centre as we know it today: A place for men, women, and children from all walks of life to study and grow together. We began to teach things that were unheard of in the Rav's traditional circles. Our mission was to create spirituality that was palatable for the whole world but did not lose the essence, the origins of spirituality, which came through teachings of the Bible, the *Zohar*, and kabbalistic masters.

The Rav and I studied the teachings of Shabbatai Donnolo (a 10th century Italian kabbalist, physician, writer and astrologer), the *Sefer Yetzirah* (*Book of Formation*), written by Abraham the Patriarch, which describes the astrological formation and influence of the months of the year, as well as the works of Rav Isaac Luria (the Ari), author of *Gate of Reincarnations*. We gathered these aspects of spiritual wisdom and discovered that they not only expanded people's thoughts but also helped them to understand their nature and the individual work of the soul. Together, we created a place where people could openly learn this wisdom. We believed that this generation was ready for the tools we were sharing. And that was our path.

After we grew substantially, from six people to hundreds and then to thousands, we moved into another phase. It was no longer the time for people to simply learn wisdom from a teacher; we needed to help people become more self-sustaining, independent in their study and growth. This is the evolution that is happening now, at this time.

I do not consider myself anyone's mentor. I can offer the material, but in this generation, people can connect directly to the wisdom, rather than have a teacher guiding them to a specific lifestyle. It's not the teacher; it's the teachings. The Kabbalah Centre has expanded more than ever before. We have crossed the world with Kabbalah, helping people apply this wisdom and these principles to their life.

So as the spiritual director of The Kabbalah Centre, my role is not to be the teacher but to be the spark, if you will. To be the voice that says, "This is what you can do for yourself."

It is my hope that this book, and the messages in it, will awaken and nourish your desire for connection to the Light of the Creator, as well as the Light within.

TABLE OF CONTENTS

POWER
Understand Your Life's Purpose to Achieve Your Full Potential

The Path to Discovering and Reaching Our Purpose 3
Move Forward 6
Find the Joy in Growth 8
You Have a Chance for a New Beginning 10
Remember the Power Beyond You 14
Sail Through the Chaos 16
Make a Lasting Impact in the World 18
Listen to the Whispers of Your Soul 20
Be Fruitful 22
See Difficulties as a Chance to Change 24
Know Things are for Your Highest Good 27
What Goes Around, Comes Around 31
Understand the Soul's Journey 34
Reveal Your Ultimate Potential 35
It is Never Too Late 37

SPIRITUAL WORK
Find True Fulfillment Through Self-Transformation

Now is the Time 43
Break Through Challenges 45

Practice Active Surrender 47
Find Your Way to the Next Level 50
Develop Your Intuition 52
Embrace Constant Change 54
Own Your Power 56
Accept Your Process 61
Have Certainty That Things Will Get Better 64
You Can Make Miracles 67
Remember Your Greatest Enemy is Within 70
Decline Bribes of the Soul 72
The Answer Should Be Simple 74
Understand Blessings and Curses 76
What You Say Creates Your Future 78
Angels Can be Proven by You 79
A Meditation to Defy Gravity 80
A Meditation to Welcome the Sabbath 82
The "Right" Way to Pray 84

RELATIONSHIPS
Relate to Others as a Divine Spark of God

There is Power in Community 89
Grow Closer to the Light 92
Living by Rote Suffocates Our Light 94
Practice Different Kinds of Forgiveness 96
Make Room for God 99
We Only Have a Snapshot in Time 101
Love is Oneness 103
Satisfy Your Deepest Desires 104
Parent, Know Thyself 105

Reveal Your Greatness 109
Feel the Pain of Others 111
Inject Sharing into Your Life 114

LIGHT
Rise Above the Darkness to Be the Light

Rise Above the Darkness 119
Conquer Oppression 121
There is a Light that Binds Amid Disaster 122
Creating Light for Ourselves and the World 124
Waking Up 126
There is an Alternative to Pain and Suffering – Part 1 127
There is an Alternative to Pain and Suffering – Part 2 129
Creating Blessings for Us and the World 131
Attain *Binah* Consciousness 133
Be a Child of God 135
The Gift of Rav Isaac Luria (the Ari) 138
The Light of Rav Shimon Bar Yochai 140

LOVE
Cultivate the Power of an Open Heart

See with a Good Eye 145
Open Your Heart 147
Heart Chakra Visualization 149
Be the Consciousness of Love 151

POWER

Understand Your Life's Purpose to Achieve Your
Full Potential

THE PATH TO DISCOVERING AND REACHING OUR PURPOSE

So many people today are asking, "What is my purpose and what does the Creator want for me?"

Truth be told, as long as we are alive, there is always more that the Creator wants for us. And yet, we have all experienced moments when our life feels monotonous, where it seems we are not doing anything significant or our work is unfulfilling. We feel stuck. When this is the case, it is possible that we are meant to be traveling down a different path.

When we are doing the same job day in and day out and we feel we have satisfied our duty and should not have to do more, we are keeping ourselves stagnant. One way we can choose the best path for our soul, and for a life with greater purpose, is to allow ourselves the room to explore, the time to really listen to our hearts, and the permission to think outside the box. The problem is that sometimes we stop thinking and just go through the motions. We do not check in with ourselves. Caught up in the responsibilities of life, we lose sight of our dreams. We forget to look for new ways to give more to others and do the things we already do even better.

When we take the initiative to grow, we begin the process to elevate to our next level. Finding and fulfilling our purpose is something we choose; it is not something that happens automatically. And believe me, choosing is something we need to consciously do every day by acknowledging we can do more; by looking for new ways to take on bigger challenges; by improving what we are already good at and pursuing opportunities that speak to us on a level beyond words. Reaching our purpose is a process we embark on when we realize we are not at our potential now. If we are too comfortable, then we will not move forward, and if we are breathing, then there is more we can do.

Rav Yehuda Ashlag, the founder of The Kabbalah Centre, teaches us that the universe will support the choices we make. Follow the Light, and you will always be pushed toward more Light; follow the darkness, and you will be pushed toward more darkness. We have free will to resist our selfish urges, and the more we do, the more we are able to receive the guidance that is meant to lead us down the best path. Unfortunately, sometimes we get in our own way. We forget, or do not realize, that we are the messengers and not the message, and when this happens, we tend to get the wrong calls and climb the wrong ladders. The key is to take ourselves out of the picture, and be as pure a channel as possible when listening to and helping others.

We all have an opportunity to get more clarity on the path our soul wants us to follow by tapping into what we call *Or Makif* (Surrounding Light). Simply put, Surrounding Light is the potential we can each reveal in this world.

My deepest wish for all of you, who are reading this, and everyone you will touch in your life, is that you will come to know your true purpose, have the wisdom and courage to run after it, and live your life to the fullest.

MOVE FORWARD

We are perpetually in a time of new beginnings. Just as the seasons never stop changing and time continually moves forward, the same is true with our consciousness. And yet, while we can clearly see how to move forward from one grade to the next in school or from one task to the next at work, the journey of moving forward in our spiritual work is often not so clear or easy.

To move forward spiritually means that we make choices that allow us to transcend the control of physicality by striving for something higher—the spiritual energy of our souls. This means being proactive in the way we approach our health, our relationships, our business; making changes that take us out of our present comfort zone and evolve us into more sharing beings. Asking questions of ourselves can help: Where am I going and what must I change to get there? Once we know that we need to change our bad habits, our environment, even our friends, we can either make the changes immediately or we can choose to make them another time. Most often, it is a lot easier to wait for another day or even to choose not to make the changes at all, although we know what we need to do. But by procrastinating, we are putting off the very decisions that could make a real difference in our life.

Each one of us has some positivity to share with someone else, as well as a unique potential to reveal, whether it is on a large or a small scale does not matter. But it all starts with one very important desire and the decision to move forward.

FIND THE JOY IN GROWTH

"Know from where you came, know to where you will go, and know to whom you must report."
—Akabia ben Mahalalel, *Pirkei Avot*, Chapter 3, First *Mishnah*

Perhaps we would be different people if we all followed this message. What we can understand from these words is the power of connecting to the bigger picture of our purpose. We need to remember from whence we came—the micro-speck that created life itself—and to where we will go, which is back to the micro-speck. Most importantly, we need to remember to whom we must report—our Creator. With this perspective, we have the power to stay focused on what is really relevant for our personal and global evolution. Far too often we forget that our soul's purpose has absolutely nothing to do with the extraneous things that we add into our life. Essentially, our primary reason for existence in this physical world is to play the game of life. This is a very serious and productive game, in which the challenge is to return the Light we were originally given back to its Source (the Creator) in order to make the universe whole again.

When we pay attention and we are open, we receive direction. God told Abraham, "Go from your country, your people and your father's household to the land that I will show you." (Genesis 12:1) In Kabbalah, "leaving one's house" is a code for creating a new beginning. Therefore, what we can gather here is that for Abraham to achieve his purpose as the channel of mercy for the whole world, he first needed to leave his comfort zone.

I know plenty of people who have spent their life in the same house, in the same neighborhood, with the same people. Does this mean these people have not managed to grow spiritually? Not necessarily. It is not the physical movement that is important but rather our willingness to extend ourselves beyond our customary patterns.

We need to be okay with the fact that we may not know how our day will unfold or where we will be in five years. Our work is not to know what the outcome will be but rather to know that every thought, word, and deed—positive or negative— will make a difference. Each one of us has to see what we are accountable for today, and then amend something in our personality so that in going forward we operate at a higher spiritual energy.

There is no joy in simply existing. The joy is in endeavoring, in growing, in doing things—and perhaps, sometimes, even in taking chances to find our way—while always keeping in mind who we are, what we are, and to whom we must answer.

YOU HAVE A CHANCE FOR
A NEW BEGINNING

Thank God for new beginnings, right? It is most likely that in the twenty, thirty, or fifty-plus years we have been on this planet, we have probably had hundreds of fresh starts. The ability to forget, begin anew, and see things in a different way, is the luxury of being human!

When we turn to the beginning of the Bible (Genesis) we can find many powerful secrets and lessons for us. Even within the infrastructure of the Hebrew letters that make up the word *beresheet* בראשית, the first word of the Bible, there is so much to learn. According to the great Kabbalist Rav Isaac Luria (the Ari), the Hebrew letters have a power beyond just simple transmission of language and meaning. These letters are portals through which the Light of the Creator can enter into this world. Each letter is a channel of a unique form of energy—and this is true whether or not we know how the letter sounds or how it fits into a given word.

Kabbalists also tell us that when we connect to the Hebrew letters of the prayers, we open up channels through which to send our intentions and requests.

Beresheet, which means "in the beginning," is the very first word of the Bible, the seed if you will, and it begins with the Hebrew letter *Bet* ב. The kabbalists tell us that the letter Bet represents bracha, meaning "blessing," which is the impetus that brings everything else into existence.

The letter *Bet* is also the first letter of the word *bitachon,* meaning "faith" or the ability to have trust in yourself and in the Creator. The *Bet* of *bitachon* is one of the foundation blocks for our survival in this physical world, for without faith in oneself there can be no faith in anyone else. If you do not believe that you can accomplish something, you will not take the necessary steps to get there.

The second letter in the word *beresheet* is *Resh* ר, which is the first letter of the word *ratzon,* meaning "desire." Without *ratzon* there is no life-force. It is desire that moves us forward— something that excites us when we rise in the morning, and fulfills us when we go to sleep at night. Without motivation, we cannot have real fulfillment in life. To draw motivation and build our desire, we can connect to the letter *Resh.*

The third letter is *Alef* א, which begins the word *ahava* or "love." Can you picture this world without love? Can you imagine life without love? Not the romantic kind of love between two people, though that is beautiful, but love of the Creator and Creation—the love that comes from looking at a flower with awe and wonder, knowing that only the Lightforce could have created such splendor and perfection. Love is knowing that every single thing that lives, breathes, and grows has a purpose; from the gnat to the human being, everything is created in synchronicity and with purpose.

Next is the letter *Shin* 𐤔, which is the first letter of the word *sheket* or "peace and quiet." How many of us find the quiet within? For us to live, we must breathe in before we can breathe out. To grow we also need to go to that place within where it is quiet enough for us to question: What have I done, who am I becoming, and what do I need to change?

The final letter of the word Beresheet is the *Taf* 𐤕, which leads us back to the word *Torah*, because without a guide to understanding and purpose, how can there be meaning and fulfillment in what we do? If we do not have spiritual awareness, then to steal, rob, hurt, or endanger others, to act without human dignity is all fair game, and the world would cease to exist.

The *Taf* is also the first letter of the word *teshuvah*. Now what does *teshuvah* really mean? Usually the word is translated as "repentance," but essentially *teshuvah* is "a return," a return to the beginning or a return to our essence, that spark of the Creator inside of us. This world was formed with the concept of human dignity, and with the ability to forgive and change. *Teshuvah* means that we are imbued with the ability to do our little part to be deserving of the Light that God had given us.

In the word *beresheet*, we find a portal to the energy of new beginnings. Through its power we can get a fresh start, turn a new page. I believe each one of us needs another beginning regardless of how old we are or what we have done before.

One of my favorite expressions is "God put erasers on pencils." The sweet spiritual truth is that mistakes and their correction are both woven into the fabric of the universe because the Creator knows and loves His children.

REMEMBER THE POWER BEYOND YOU

"Do not forget the Lord your God by not keeping His commandments, His judgments, and His statues."
—Deuteronomy 8:11

"Beware lest you say in your heart 'My strength and the might of my hand that has accumulated this wealth for me.'"
—Deuteronomy 8:17

What we learn from this precept is to awaken our consciousness and understand that there is no blessing without the help of the Light. When we achieve something or reach a successful place, we should not believe it was our power alone that brought us here.

The *Zohar*, in the portion of Bamidbar 1:11, tells us, "Come and Behold: he who speaks in praise of his friend, of his children, of his money or wealth, must also bless the Creator and acknowledge those blessings."

The *Zohar* explains that the Creator does not need our blessings, and that "bless the Creator," means to be aware of the Force beyond our own power that propels our path to success. However, due to the nature of this physical world, we can forget. Pride overrides our awareness and appreciation of the Light in our life.

Within the 72 Names of God, we find all of the Hebrew letters but one—the letter *Gimel* גּ, which represents *ga'ava* or "pride." When we are proud of our accomplishments and *our* work, there is no awareness and, therefore, no presence of the Light in our actions.

So at times when we are full with our own ego, full with some kind of condescending attitude toward people, we have totally forgotten why we came here in the first place, and the fact that each and every one of us is capable of transforming who we are in the moment by saying, "Thank you, Creator, for allowing me to be who I am."

SAIL THROUGH THE CHAOS

The Creator did not promise that we would have a life free of chaos. There was no guarantee that we would not lose someone dear to us; nor was there a promise that life would be one big party—this is not the reason why we have incarnated into this world. We incarnate to engage with the chaos, and use our consciousness, effort, and actions to transform it into Light.

If we have faith in our spirituality, we will come to understand that no matter what darkness falls before us, it is there for a reason—to help us grow and change—and our problems, and the situations we are in, are a result of something we have done, whether in this lifetime or a prior lifetime.

It is written in the Bible: *Vayehi erev vayehi boker*, which means, "And there was night, and there was morning." The reason night is mentioned first is because without the darkness we could not understand polarity, and we could not know the Light.

How many of us have found the joy of spirituality only after having undergone some test of fire? It is as if at some point in our life the Creator gives us a whammy and says, "You are running out of time. Get to your point." We are brought dark situations so that eventually we can discover the Light.

We have all experienced some form of chaos at one time or another and possibly asked, "How can this be happening to me? I learn, I study, I pray, and sometimes I even give to charity. I am a good person. I have done all of these good things. Why is my life not smooth?" There is an African proverb that answers this: "Smooth seas do not make skillful sailors."

We are not on this Earth just to sail through our short years. Each of us has been gifted with an opportunity, and our time on this planet is to take what we have been given and consciously use it to reveal Light.

MAKE A LASTING IMPACT IN THE WORLD

During the lifetime of illustrious people, we seldom appreciate having them around or understand what they do. Sadly, it is usually after they leave us that we realize their worth and merit.

The Bible tells us that Sarah lived to the age of 127. (Genesis 23:1) At 100, she was as beautiful as a 20-year-old, and as pure as a seven-year-old. Although she had lived many years, she was youthful in spirit; the Light inside of her was not diminished.

Although people age, if you look at those who continuously take positive actions in life, you will notice they always seem to have the strength and enthusiasm to fulfill the people around them.

On a cold New York evening, one of our Kabbalah Centre teachers was driving with his children. His young son looked out the window and saw someone on the side of the road wandering without shoes. The boy said, "Daddy stop, we have to help this man!" His father responded, "What do you want me to do?" His son said, "Give him your shoes." And so the teacher stopped the car and gave the man his shoes.

Now I am not saying that we all need to take off our shoes every time we see a vagrant walking around without a pair.

But through the pure eyes of a child we can understand that actions of kindness, of extending ourselves for others, is what gives energy to life.

The things we strive for in this world—money, position, and respect—are, in and of themselves, nothing. In the end, the only real and lasting impact we make is when we positively affect the lives of others. Money, position, and respect can be tools that help us in this mission but they cannot be our end goal, for in and of themselves they do not last. Everything in this physical world is impermanent and transitory—everything, that is, except for the love and the care we can share.

Every day we live is like a basket that we fill with our actions. If we go through the day consistently gathering garbage, we will have a basket full of garbage at the end of the day. On the other hand, if we fill our basket with positive actions that increase the Light in the life of others, then, when the day is done, we will have a basket full of energy that will never fade. The choice is ours.

LISTEN TO THE WHISPERS OF YOUR SOUL

"No longer will they teach their neighbor, or say to one another, 'Know the Lord,' because they will all know Me, from the least of them to the greatest."
—Jeremiah 31:34

At times we all fall into a consciousness of going through the motions—of being preoccupied with the details of life. We work, we eat, we breathe, we sleep, and then we get up the next morning and do it all over again. Have we not all at some point thought this is just the way life is?

There are other times, however, when we wake to the question: What is all of this really about? After all, I have lived a solid life and still, I do not feel fulfilled. There must be a more profound aspect to this physical existence, something else I can learn, something more I can do to bring greater meaning to life.

When we reach this place—this moment of desire for truth—we have reached a soul evolution, a new understanding of why we came into this world. We begin to realize that we are not here simply to go through the motions. A soul evolution is usually earned by overcoming some sort of challenge—a test of fire. Or in some cases it can come as a gentle whisper, "Wake up, wake up. Life is more than what you can see."

According to the kabbalists, more and more people will begin to achieve this spiritual maturity as we come closer to the time when the Lightforce of the Creator becomes more revealed in our physical dimension.

BE FRUITFUL

Our soul has to be cultivated and nurtured to be fruitful. Most of the time we are so busy doing things to satisfy the desires of the body, that we do not give ourselves time to see the beauty that is inside; the time to talk to our soul and listen to what it wants for us.

The Bible portion of Vayak'hel opens with Moses addressing the people about *Shabbat*. Moses says, "Work may be performed during the six weekdays. However, on the seventh, refrain from all labor." (*Midrash, Shemot*) Shabbat, the day we rest our desire to fulfill our physical well-being, is a time to allow the Light inside of us to do its work. We are not required to do anything physical; we simply welcome the spiritual essence within us to be. It is a day when we honor that part of ourselves that is connected directly to the Creator. On *Shabbat*, we are no longer involved with the mundane, so we create a space for the Light to come in and ignite our soul.

The Creator did not put us on this Earth to simply live, reproduce, and die. He gave us a specific job: To make the world a better place. This does not mean we all have to become activists; it means we need to nurture our soul so it can be fruitful.

In Deuteronomy 30:19, the Creator says, "I call on Heaven and Earth to witness against you today that I have presented you with life and death, the blessing and the curse. Therefore, choose life, so that you will live..."

The paradox of life is that when we think of satisfying only ourselves, we can never be satisfied. If we eat the best meal in the world all alone, then one day, one week, or one month later, not only will it no longer satisfy us, we will not even remember it. However, if we eat a decent meal with the best company, and we share wonderful energy, a conversation, or give or receive some good advice, we will continue to be fulfilled by this experience forever. This is why it is written in the *Zohar*, "Have as much as you can, just make sure that when you receive something you also give something." This is not about morality; it is a technology to fulfill our hungry soul.

After one hundred and twenty years, when we go upstairs, there will be no record of how many houses we owned or how many contracts we closed. All that will be known about us is how many people were better off because we existed. No more and no less.

Our job is to help our soul be fruitful by sharing with others; this is the purpose of our life. Otherwise, we could simply have been born animals. But we are human, and we connect to the Lightforce by giving from the bounty of our soul.

SEE DIFFICULTIES AS A CHANCE TO CHANGE

Who are the people we call heroes? They are the individuals who, when presented with a dark situation, find the internal fortitude, passion, and perseverance to create something positive. So many of these men and women go unrecognized in their efforts to make things better for their neighbors— and even for strangers. Sadly, natural and manmade disasters are often the setting from which such heroes spring. Indeed, history teaches us that most of humanity's most notable accomplishments have blossomed from the seeds of hard work and persistence sown on behalf of others in the face of difficulty.

The Bible teaches us about the enormous potential of human nature in the face of adversity through the life of Abraham. He reached his greatness because of how he passed through his ten trials: Assassins tried to murder him when he was an infant; he was imprisoned for ten years; he had to leave his home and migrate to Canaan; a famine drove him to Egypt; Pharaoh took his wife Sarah; he battled an alliance of eastern kings; he experienced a vision and performed a sacrifice that sealed his "covenant"; he was circumcised; his son Ishmael tried to kill his other son Isaac; and finally, God asked Abraham to sacrifice his son Isaac.

For many people, each of these tests alone would be too much to endure. Yet it was not simply Abraham's endurance of the trials that made him great; it was the way he responded to them. He did not complain in the face of each difficulty or say, "Why do I have to do this? Why am I being forced to suffer in this way?" Instead, whatever the Creator asked of him, Abraham accepted as his role with certainty. He took each circumstance he was given and worked with it to create something of beauty. Whatever seemed negative, he transformed into something positive.

How many times does life throw us a curve ball and the first thing we think is: Why me? After all, am I not a spiritual person? Oftentimes, we approach our day as a series of tasks to complete: Wake up, go to work, do whatever we need to do to get on with our lives. If we complete these tasks, we are happy and feel productive; if we do not, we are left feeling dissatisfied.

Abraham approached his day differently. Each time he met with aggression or a person that sought to do him harm, every wall he encountered or change he had to face, he accepted for the gift that was in it. In other words, instead of being a victim, Abraham lived to find the spirituality in each day, in each trial, in each frustration that he faced.

We do not have to wait for tragedy to strike to become the hero of our own lives. When someone or some situation challenges us, we have a choice. We can think: How can I make this situation go away as soon as possible? Or we can think: How can I transform this situation into Light? In quickly pushing uncomfortable things aside, we can miss the opportunity being presented for us to grow.

If we open our eyes and tune in spiritually, we will find that each day affords us with the chance to discover the light from the darkness.

KNOW THINGS ARE FOR YOUR HIGHEST GOOD

A young Rabbi, Yochanan ben Levi, prayed to God that he might be given permission to observe the prophet Elijah. God granted his prayer, and Elijah appeared to him. Speaking from his heart, he asked, "Elijah, may I journey with you for just a short time and watch all that you do, bringing miracles to the world and serving the Creator?"

To this Elijah replied, "Yes, you may, but with one condition: Please do not ask questions. Just observe."

Rabbi Yochanan agreed, and the two men set out on their journey to a small town.

Their first destination was a poor family whose entire livelihood came from one single cow. Elijah and Rabbi Yochanan visited with the family and stayed for the night. In the morning, Elijah prayed, and the only cow, which brought sustenance to the family, died. Baffled and confused, Rabbi Yochanan began to question what Elijah had done to this poor family. Seeing his bewilderment, Elijah reminded him firmly, "No questions." And with that, the two continued on their way.

Their next visit was to the house of a very wealthy but ungracious man. From the moment they knocked on his door, they were treated with disdain and a complete lack of human dignity. Their unkind host made no apologies for this behavior; in fact, he stated, "Since you are here, I will feed you but you can only stay in the servants' quarters. I will give you bread and water, not because I welcome you but because I must follow the foolish social custom that demands it of me."

Soon after they had rested a bit and had eaten some bread, Elijah and Rabbi Yochanan prepared to thank their host and depart. As they were leaving, Elijah blessed the host, "I see that the walls of your house are crumbling. Out of gratitude for your hospitality, I will pay for a contractor to repair them." The rabbi was baffled by Elijah's generosity but he refrained from asking any questions.

The prophet and the rabbi then approached a community full of callous people who snubbed the two men as soon as they arrived. And once again, to Rabbi Yochanan's amazement, Elijah gave them all a great blessing, "May you each be a leader in your own right."

With this, Rabbi Yochanan's frustration with Elijah grew stronger. Why did he slaughter the cow that belonged to a man who had treated them with such kindness and humility, and then bless their rude host and this community filled with ego and pride? Nevertheless, the rabbi had promised not to ask questions, so he kept silent and followed Elijah to their next destination.

The next community was a modest one, filled with wonderful people who served Elijah and Rabbi Yochanan with grace and hospitality. When the time came for them to be on their way, Elijah turned to the head of the community and said, "I pray that you have one leader."

Upon hearing this, Rabbi Yochanan could no longer keep his tongue silent, "Please, I just can't take this anymore. I don't understand what is happening, can you explain it to me?"

Elijah agreed. "I will share with you why I did what I did. At the first home we visited, there was a decree that the poor man's wife was meant to pass away that day, so in my prayers I asked that the cow be taken instead, and God answered my prayers.

"Hidden beneath the wealthy man's house was a fortune that was not meant for him. Had he begun construction, he would have discovered the treasure and gained even more wealth and power, so I paid for a contractor to repair the house so the owner would never find the hidden money.

"As for the residents of the wealthy, arrogant community, my blessing for them was that every one of them should be a leader. Do you know what happens when you have a community of leaders and no followers? You have no community at all; it tears itself apart.

"In the last town we visited, I wished the townsfolk harmony, unity, love, and strength that comes with only one leader."

All at once, Rabbi Yochanan understood why everything had happened the way it did. It was as if a curtain was lifted and he was able to see the reasons for all that had appeared to occur before him.

Can you imagine if we could have the curtain lifted on our own lives?

Very often, we cannot, and do not, see why things are as they are because our perspective is limited. By staying open to possibility and connecting to the bigger picture, we can understand that even the most difficult and painful things are for our highest good and to help us attain our next level of spiritual growth.

POWER
Understand Your Life's Purpose to Achieve Your Full Potential

WHAT GOES AROUND, COMES AROUND

Rav Isaac Luria (the Ari) discusses the many reincarnations of our teachers in the volume of the *Writings of the Ari: Gate of Reincarnations*. Every word found in his writings is meant to teach us something and awaken our consciousness about the workings of this world. Why does the Ari say so much about reincarnation? What difference does it make if we know about reincarnation or even believe in it, for that matter? Because if we can understand what we came back to learn, we can fix it. By fixing it, we can heal the chaos in our lives and, eventually, do our part to heal the chaos in the world.

The Rav would say, "Knowledge is the connection, and awareness proceeds change. To solve a problem, I need to first become fully cognizant that it exists. Denial is the food of inaction."

There is a story about a student of the famed 18th century Kabbalist, the Baal Shem Tov (Rav Israel ben Eliezer), who asked his master, "Is there justice in this world?" To which the Baal Shem Tov replied, "Tomorrow afternoon, go to the park, take a seat, and observe what you see around you."

Following his teacher's instruction, the next day the student visited the park, found a nice place to sit down, and looked around. Sure enough a young man carrying a valise appeared. He seemed very happy, and sat down on a park bench to rest for a moment and bask in the sunlight. Suddenly his expression changed. It was as if he had forgotten something, and he leapt to his feet and ran off. In his preoccupation with what troubled him, he left his valise beside the bench where he set it down. Several minutes later, an older man walked by and noticed the valise on the ground. He picked it up, placed it on the bench and opened it. Inside there were wads of money. The older man's obvious excitement took his breath away; he looked around anxiously, every which way, and not seeing anyone coming to claim it, took off with the valise full of money!

Only minutes later, a third man came along and sat down on the bench to relax and enjoy the afternoon. The young man returned and feverishly looked for his missing valise. Not seeing it, he turned to the man sitting on the bench and barked at him, "Where is my valise? What have you done with my valise and my money?" The third man, shaken from his quietude answered, "What valise? There was no valise here, and I have no idea what money you are talking about." Infuriated by his loss, the young man accused, "You took my valise; I left it right there next to this bench. You must have taken it. Give it back!" The young man beat upon the third man, who threw out a few punches in defense as well. Finally, exasperated and exhausted, the young man walked away.

The student was more bewildered than ever. The next day, he returned to the Baal Shem Tov, and said to his teacher, "After what I saw, and after much consideration, I have come to understand there is no justice in this world and that we must wait for the World to Come." The Baal Shem Tov replied, "Tell me what you saw." The student recollected what he had seen at the park and how he had arrived at his conclusion.

The Baal Shem Tov answered with the following, "King David was right when he said, 'We have eyes but do not see, and ears but do not hear.' Clearly the scene at the park tells the story of a past lifetime. You see the first man and the second man were business partners. The first man stole money from his partner, the second man. Now, in this life, the second man has taken his money back."

After beginning to see more of the picture, the student inquired, "But what about the third man who was beaten for simply sitting at the bench?" The Baal Shem Tov explained, "He was the judge who ruled in favor of the thieving partner in that past life."

The lesson the Baal Shem Tov shared with his student, and with us, is that there is no situation in life, no scene playing out that is random. The cosmos is a perfect algorithm; it does not make mistakes. We do.

UNDERSTAND THE SOUL'S JOURNEY

Once upon a time, there were two caterpillars who were the best of friends; they spent all of their time together, doing the things that caterpillars do. Every morning, they would meet and begin new adventures. One morning, the older of the two caterpillars did not arrive. The other caterpillar looked everywhere but could not find her friend. After some time, she simply realized her friend was not coming back, and this saddened her. Crying, she looked up and saw a beautiful butterfly coming to sit next to her. The butterfly said, "Why are you crying? I have not left you, I have just transformed into a butterfly."

In coming to terms with immortality, we grow to understand that the soul takes on different forms throughout its many incarnations. Although we might miss those that are dear to us, they are simply experiencing the next evolution in the journey of their soul.

REVEAL YOUR ULTIMATE POTENTIAL

The Netziv (Rav Naphtali Tzvi Judah Berlin) was a great sage who lived during the 1800s. He was a financial genius, very active in all matters of monetary endeavors, and he was known to invest much of his time devising ways to grow his wealth. Yet with all that he had, he was not a very giving person.

One night, the Netziv had a dream. In it, he saw two angels talking; one angel said to the other, "Should we show him all that he is meant to achieve—all that he is not doing—in this lifetime?"

The other angel replied, "Yes, let us open the curtain and show him." And with that they opened the curtain, and all the books the Netziv was destined to write and all the people he was intended to influence with his spiritual wisdom became evident.

In the dream, the Netziv saw a luminous white angel sitting at the bottom of the Throne of God, and the angel asked him, "Where are the books? Where are the spiritual works you are destined to accomplish and all the people you are going to reach through your writings?"

He saw himself replying, "You know, I had so many things in the works..."

The angel of God said, "Do you think God gave you such a great mind to acquire a sack of gold? Do you think that gaining wealth is the reason why He put you in this world?"

Upon waking from his disturbing dream, the Netziv vowed to fulfill his purpose as the angels had revealed to him.

The following night, the Netziv had another dream; the angels came to him again and said, "Blessed are you in this world and the next." The Netziv, following through on his commitment, went on to establish a school with many students, and he wrote numerous books. His students passed on the Netziv's story throughout the generations to teach us a valuable lesson about fulfilling our purpose in this lifetime. The most important task before each of us is to always ask what is our mission, and then go ahead and fulfill it.

IT IS NEVER TOO LATE

There are those who, at middle age or even older, after having achieved so much, find that they want or need to make a change. Leonardo da Vinci was a military engineer and architect before he painted the Mona Lisa and the Last Supper. Ronald Reagan was a movie actor before he entered politics, became governor of California and then president of the United States. These late life changes often lead to accomplishing more than the initial path could have afforded.

From the Bible, we understand that Abraham was 100 years old when he became the spiritual leader of a nation. (Genesis 18:10-12) We may consider this to be a dramatic life change to undergo at such advanced age, after all, have we never heard or even said, "Change? Me? I'm too old for that!" Truth be told, history supports the fact that no matter how old we are or how far we think we have progressed, an opportunity is always before us to break out of our comfort zone and accept responsibility for the Light we have brought to share with the world.

Each of us has been allotted a certain amount of time, and ability in the physical body that houses our soul, to do good deeds. Yet time and again, when a new challenge is handed to us, we shy away from it and say, "I am not ready for it" or "I have already done that" or "I do not trust this is the way I should go." In response to these questions, the universe, in turn, asks: "What will push this person to the wall so the Light inside of him can be drawn out and shared with the world? How can I bring this person to change?"

Abraham was one of the most gifted astrologers of all time. According to what he saw in the stars, he believed that he would have no children. We know, of course, that he did. The Creator told Abraham that the stars impel but they do not compel. Because of Abraham's spiritual transformation—at the age of 100—he was able to change his destiny.

It is important for us to know that we can change the direction of our lives; not everything mapped out in the Heavens is required to play out. For example, we accept it as fact that the Earth rotates around the Sun. Yet it is written in Joshua 10:13: "Then spoke Joshua to the Lord in the day when the Lord delivered up the Amorites before the children of Israel; and he said in the sight of Israel: 'Sun, stand you still upon Gibeon; and you, Moon, in the Valley of Aijalon.' So the sun stood still, and the moon stopped."

We learn that the Creator made an exception: Everything in the natural world that is certain and fixed was charged not to be so. It is the same for us. We are born with a charted course but that course can be altered based on our consciousness, words, and actions.

There is no such decree as, "This is how my life will be," because we have the power to change it.

SPIRITUAL
WORK

Find True Fulfillment Through
Self-Transformation

NOW IS THE TIME

Quite often we ask the Creator to fulfill our desire, to give us "something" that we want: The girl, the guy, the house, the child, the career, the well-being we desire, even the miracle we need. Usually when we ask, we want it now!

What about what the Creator asks of us? What about our spiritual work? What about becoming the person each of us is meant to be? When it is our turn to deliver on our potential, we usually say something like: "Yes, of course I will change; I will resist getting angry. But God, remember, change does not happen overnight. Give me time."

Why then, do we expect the Creator to give us what we ask for, instantly, if we are not making the changes we need to make, now? The Creator acts as our mirror: What we put out is what we get back, measure for measure. If we are immediate in all that we are meant to do, then the Creator will be immediate in what we ask. However, if there is a lapse between our decision and our action, then we can expect there will be a lapse in the Creator's response to us.

If we want the Creator to be fast to answer, then we to need to be quick to act. If we have a problem with anger, in the heat of the moment we might have been inclined to cut ourselves some slack believing our wrath was justified by the situation. Instead, we could decide: "Now I am going to be different, and from this moment forward, things will be different."

Every situation offers an opportune time to start a new page, a new chapter. Because, spiritually speaking, every day that we are not moving forward with our transformation, we are actually falling backward.

Each of us has a soul that is in exile from the Light because of our reactive system. However, we were also created with the capacity to overcome it right now. When we do, we are living up to the condition to ask for what we want right now.

BREAK THROUGH CHALLENGES

When Pharaoh let the Israelites leave Egypt, it is written that, "God led the people by way of the wilderness to the Red Sea." We are told there was a shorter way, so why did God choose the longer route? God said, "The people might change their minds when they see war, and return to Egypt." (Exodus 13:17) Though the longer path had more severe hardships, it nonetheless prevented the people from finding their way back to Egypt.

What a strange concept. Why would the people want to return to the land of their slavery? Clearly Egypt did not represent a country but a consciousness, and God's route was not purely geographical; it was a spiritual route. The lesson here is to understand that achieving a higher level of consciousness, a level that leaves personal slavery behind, means venturing into the unknown. In the same way the Israelites wanted to return to Egypt, we often prefer to go back to our own "Egypt," where we feel safe, even if it means going back to chaos. For at least in our own Egypt it feels familiar; we know what to expect. Traveling a new route, we have no idea what will come before us or what the end result might be. For our own benefit, sometimes the Creator has to lead us away and onto the unexpected path because this prevents us from returning to the chaos we left behind.

Although we may all want to stay on our spiritual path and live up to our commitments, life gets in the way, challenges arise, and pretty soon it can seem easier to go back to where we started. When this happens, we need to remember that every challenge we encounter is part of the Creator's design to help us grow and change. The more arduous the path, the more opportunity it affords us to mend our ways. The more negativity in a situation, the more potential there is to reveal Light.

Are we committed to escaping our personal Egypt? The route is set—the task is to leave our slavery behind, move forward, and not look back.

PRACTICE ACTIVE SURRENDER

There is a kind of surrender when we call out to the Creator and say, "I give myself to you! I let go." This is a passive surrender. There is another form of surrender—active surrender. With active surrender, I am prepared to apply what I have learned and am willing *to do* whatever I have to do to achieve spiritual elevation. This means disengaging from old habits of being a victim and actively shifting my mind from believing that things *just happen* to the deep internal knowing that nothing, but nothing, just happens.

Active surrender is the unshakable certainty that comes from doing spiritual work. When life throws me a curveball, I surrender with an active awareness that this curve ball is perfect, giving me exactly what I need right now. I know I say this a lot, in different ways, and the reason is that developing this kind of spiritual alignment takes tremendous practice and repetition. With active surrender, there is no doubt, nor is there an intellectual understanding. There is only a knowing that what is happening now is either a result of something I did in this lifetime or in a prior one, or that this specific situation, with all of its twists and turns, is meant to lead me to a better version of myself.

Active surrender does not come from a point of failure. Active surrender means having certainty in spite of the seeming chaos; it is experiencing the light within the darkness. Even in the face of illness, bankruptcy, broken family relations, we actively persevere: "I accept and surrender my being to a higher power that will bring me from this to something better." Even though we may not know the reasons why, we surrender with certainty.

In the Bible, we find Joseph as the conduit of *Yesod*, one of the spiritual levels on the kabbalistic Tree of Life. The Tree of Life has 10 levels or *Sefirot*, and each level is a different emanation of the Lightforce of God. *Yesod* hovers just above the lowest level, *Malchut*, our physical world, and is the channel of spiritual abundance that brings Light from the Upper World to the darkness of the physical world. Joseph's life was a tale of active surrender; he met with every act of unfairness and betrayal with dignity and grace. When his brothers sold him as a slave, he became controller of the servants of a prominent household. When he was unjustly arrested and sent to the dungeon, he became valued there. Eventually, he earned all the abundance and all the Light that was his destiny. No matter the situation, he rose to the top, like oil; never losing trust in the Light's path for him. He maintained strength and certainty with the knowledge that wherever he was, whatever was done to him, there was a reason for it. This consciousness of active surrender, in the face of the Creator's chiseling tool, formed him into an eternal channel for abundance for all of humanity.

When the Creator's hand comes to form our strength, let us actively work to know that there is a bigger plan and a reason for whatever position we are in. With active surrender, we can rise to the top of any situation and discover our destiny, even if things do not appear to be going our way.

FIND YOUR WAY TO THE NEXT LEVEL

In the biblical portion of Lech Lecha, the Creator tells Abraham to leave his home, yet does not inform him on where to go. (Genesis 12:1) If God were directing Abraham to move, why would God not also tell him where he should go?

Spiritually, every human being is internally connected to his or her next level, with a deep knowing of where he or she is meant to go in this life. Although the Light is ever-present for us, if a person is stuck, or tied to something and unable to let go, it is up to the individual to look inside and figure out what the next step needs to be. This is why the sages of Kabbalah tell us there can be no coercion in spirituality. For us to earn the Light, the decision has to be our own. We are each responsible for taking action and forging direction in our lives.

The question is: If the Creator doesn't tell us where to go, then how can we know how to get to the next level?

When we know that we can do something more than we are doing now, and then a door opens for us, we know this is the door we are meant to walk through.

God is always there, knocking on our door, telling us to go to another level and to become more than who we are.

Are we listening—or are we limiting ourselves, staying in a place that may not be the best for us because it is comfortable?

DEVELOP YOUR INTUITION

Developing intuition means developing our listening skills—listening to others and to our own inner voice. It is a different kind of work than we are used to. Our society tends to focus more on external communication, such as speaking and writing, and less on internal skills like listening.

Intuition grows when we embrace our internal nature and then go beyond personal worries, fears, and agendas. It grows when we learn to take ourselves out of the situation, seeing things as an observer rather than as a participant, while at the same time feeling empathy for others.

When we are in a space of intuition, we work from the Third Eye Chakra, which sits right between the eyebrows on the forehead. Through this energy center, we can direct energy throughout our entire body. We allow ourselves to operate from an internal place rather than from external forces, such as what others think or expect of us. The more we can do this, then absolutely, the more intuitive we become.

Operating from intuitive awareness is a humble bow to the understanding that we are each a piece of energy that has come to this world in a physical body. The Light that we can share and be a part of, is not ours alone—it is the energy that connects us all as one soul; it is the energy that breathes life into all that exists. In and of ourselves alone, we are finite.

By asking the Creator to help us open this Third Eye to see with kindness and inspiration, we can create an empathy between ourselves and those around us, know when to say the right things, and how to feel the pain of others so that we can help them.

It is really important, especially in this day and age, that the awakening that comes to our spiritual growth is allowed to enter through this Third Eye Chakra and into the rest of our being.

EMBRACE CONSTANT CHANGE

"On the twentieth day of the second month of the second year, the cloud lifted from above the Tabernacle of the covenant law. Then the Israelites set out from the Desert of Sinai and traveled from place to place until the cloud came to rest in the Desert of Paran. They set out, this first time, at the Lord's command through Moses."
—Numbers 10:11-13

"Let's move forward!" Moses said to the Israelites after they had been at Mount Sinai for just over two years. Why did Moses want them to leave? Mount Sinai was one of the holiest, most Light-filled spiritual locations. It was where the world was offered the totality of spiritual energy through the giving of the Torah—the greatest revelation of Light of all time. Still, Moses said: "Let's go, let's move forward!"

The Bible teaches us this lesson in many ways, through various stories, and the lesson cannot be repeated often enough. We may believe we are where we belong, however, to grow, we have to leave it all behind, although it might be difficult and seem unreasonable.

Generally, we do not see where we need to be right away, and it can take years to become obvious. Essentially, there is a level of consciousness that we grow into before we can have perspective on where we were and what we have still to do to develop. This is not something we can be taught; it is simply an evolution of consciousness that we can only understand when looking back. Like a teenager looking at a one-year-old, there is only so much you can teach an infant about walking and talking; it is simply a developmental process that does not have a shortcut. Consciousness works the same way; we cannot be taught a new level of consciousness before our time.

We learn through circumstances that push us out of our land, our comfort zone, our consciousness, and even areas that are full of Light. This can be so painful, but this is how we grow and how Light is revealed through the darkness.

OWN YOUR POWER

As King David was traveling to Bahurim, along the way a man named Shimei, the son of Gera, from the same clan as King Saul's family, came out and cursed the king. He did not stop there; he also threw stones at King David and his officials. (2 Samuel 16:5-6)

One of the king's men said to him, "Let me go over and cut off his head."

King David urged him not to do so, saying, "Leave him alone. Let him curse, for if God told him to 'curse David,' it must be that I deserve it. Maybe God will look upon my misery and restore a blessing instead of this curse today." (Ibid. 11-12) King David and his men then continued on their way, while Shimei stood on the opposite mountain, still throwing stones. King David understood one of the most powerful spiritual concepts in the universe—a concept that forms the basis for all of our spiritual work on this path of Kabbalah, and which, when understood and employed in one's consciousness, has the power to change the very reality that we experience. At the same time, it is a concept that we can remember but then so quickly forget.

What is this concept?

We, you and I, each human being on the planet, are 100 percent responsible for everything we experience in our lives. Everything—the good, the bad, the beautiful, the ugly.

As the Rav wrote in his book, To the Power of One:

> *"The Zohar drives home the point that we have an orderly universe around us. But before we can move ahead and access this universe, we must first rid ourselves of the belief that we are helpless human beings aboard a rudderless ship in a stormy sea. We can and must assure ourselves that we, and we alone, will master the future course of our life experiences. Life is not a game of chance. Chance is but an illusion."*

Most of us are accepting of this concept when it comes to taking responsibility for our words and behavior. We are good at saying, "Okay, I did it and now I am dealing with the effects of what I did." However, the responsibility that I am talking about is more comprehensive than that.

When we get angry and snap at people, refuse to extend human dignity to the people around us or do not care about things as we should, we create a little ball of negative energy that does not disappear. The law of conservation of energy, discovered by Julius Robert Mayer in 1842, tells us that energy cannot be destroyed, it simply changes form. The negative energy we create through our reactivity sits someplace in the computer called our life, and generally we do not feel its presence until it boomerangs into our experience in the form of some sort of chaos. Even then, we may or may not know when or what we did to create it, because it is a result of something we did inadvertently or in another lifetime; it is not as if we consciously put it there. But ten years hence something happens, and we could possibly find ourselves experiencing a form of judgment in our lives. We blame any number of individuals or circumstances for the judgment because we do not see that the reason we are in our current situation is a result of the data we input at another time.

When we experience chaos, confusion, anger, or hatred, it is because at some point along our way we did something to block ourselves from the Lightforce of the Creator, and we are experiencing the effect of that blockage. Although we may not identify when, why, or any specifics about the original circumstances that brought it about, nonetheless, we are back here to take responsibility, remove the curtain that blocks us, and thereby change what we experience.

A spiritual concept that is often used when describing the holiday of Yom Kippur is atonement, which *Merriam Webster's Dictionary* defines as, "reparation for an offense or injury." Kabbalistically, this concept can be understood as "at-one-ment" with the Light of the Creator. But "at-one-ment" is not reserved for only one day of the year. Rather, it is a process we are meant to engage in on a daily basis, and it is one of the single most powerful tools for changing our reality.

Every time we experience a reaction that puts us at odds with the infinite Light of pure love and sharing, we are actually being presented with a moment to come back into "at-one-ment" with the Creator. The people and situations in our lives—in all our lifetimes, in fact—are simply agents to awaken those places within us that still need to be repaired. As we do this work of repairing, more blessings, love, and energy can flow through us.

The reason why fear, anger, hatred or resentment show up within us when they do is because those moments—for reasons beyond our understanding—are the perfect time for us to take responsibility for them and free up some space on our hard drive.

The most important point of this process is to understand that atonement is not about guilt. Enough with the purging already! Self-responsibility is about freeing ourselves on a very deep level—freeing ourselves from the karmic seeds we may have planted in this lifetime or in a past life. Guilt and shame block us from truly doing this process. In fact, guilt and shame are blocks for which we need to atone for.

All the tools we utilize at The Kabbalah Centre—the *Zohar*, the 72 Names of God, the *Ana Beko'ach* prayer, even participating in events celebrating cosmic windows in time— are actually here to help us achieve this unity with the Lightforce. The Rav referred to holidays as "whole-i-days" because they are periods when we can employ specific spiritual tools, revealed by ancient kabbalists, to help us return to our original wholeness, our oneness with the Creator.

ACCEPT YOUR PROCESS

"Do what you can, with what you have, where you are."
—Theodore Roosevelt

This is a powerful lesson for our spiritual purpose here on Earth—the mission of perfecting our souls. We have been given all that we have—our traits, limitations, our gifts, our set-backs, our talents—so that we will be able to transform from within.

In the Bible portion of Va'etchanan, Moses recounts his interaction with God, "I also pleaded with God at that time, saying, 'You have begun to show Your servant Your greatness and Your strong hand; for what god is there in Heaven or on Earth who can do such works and mighty acts as Yours? Let me, I pray, cross over and see the fair land (Israel) that is beyond the Jordan, that good hill country and Lebanon.'"

As Moses relates in the very next verse, God did not grant him his aspiration: "But the Creator was angry with me on your (the Israelites) account, and would not listen to me; and God said to me, 'Enough! Speak to Me no more of this matter.'" (Deuteronomy 3:23 – 3:25).

The *Midrash* explains that Moses went on to pray 515 times for this aspiration. Interestingly, *va'etchanan* is also one of ten Hebrew words for "praying."

Why did Moses need to beg so much just to go into the land? With all that he had done for the nation, why did Moses still need to implore the Creator for this seemingly small request? When Moses' sister Miriam was sick with leprosy, Moses demanded of the Creator "Heal her now," and she was healed. How can it be that Moses could, on one hand, be arrogant and demanding and at the same time desperate to no avail?

Moses knew that he had achieved such an elevated spiritual level that, had he entered Israel, he would have brought about the perfect unification of the physical world with the spiritual world—a unification that would have resulted in global peace and the end of pain, suffering, and death. "Moses, you cannot enter the land because your action will create complete unity in the whole world. The people, however, have not yet finished correcting the negative aspects of themselves. Each person needs to go through his or her own process to complete his or her own spiritual mission. The Creator also told Moses that no person can take on another's process because each soul is a rock hewed from the same Divine mountain, each one needs to do his or her part to return to the mountain whole."

For us, this is a profound lesson. Do we reject our own process? How can we transform our limited thoughts such as: What can I do? These are my circumstances. This is the way I was born. I have no choice.

The point is that maintaining these beliefs means we put another god before us, and this god is the victim consciousness we give power to, which I like to call *victimology.*

The first of the Ten Utterances states: "I am the Lord, your God, who took you out of the land of Egypt, the house of bondage. You shall have no other gods before Me." (Exodus 20:2-3) In practice, what does this mean? When we learn Kabbalah, we discover that the Creator has given us the ability to be the cause not the effect, not a victim. "I have taken you out of your own enslavement. I have provided you with the spiritual tools to mend and create with whatever you have been given, whether it is a lot or a little."

Whatever we have for tools, we were given them by the Creator to enable us to change, as we are no longer in bondage.

There are no victims on the path of God. Enslavement is the other gods.

Regardless of our circumstances, we are always capable of applying our consciousness to become the cause, by sharing and doing our part to bring Light into this world.

HAVE CERTAINTY THAT THINGS WILL GET BETTER

All of us can be very spiritual when things are going well. But when things go wrong, it can be all too easy for us to give up. Yet when it comes to matters of a physical nature, we accept the rule of no pain, no gain; there is no substitute for hard work.

Kabbalistically, we know that physical laws of the universe mirror spiritual laws. This means that in our spiritual work as well, we must be willing to face challenges even when they appear insurmountable. Just like physical strength training, spiritual strength comes from working hard. It comes from facing difficulties put in front of us by the Creator as instruments, like weights in a gym, to help us get stronger.

To become stronger in our consciousness and grow to our next level, we need to really look at ourselves and ask the tough questions about who we are: When I reach the point where things are not what they are supposed to be, how do I react? Am I still certain of my spiritual path? Am I certain there is a bigger plan and purpose for everything, for every event or circumstance? Do I truly understand that all I have is my ability to climb the spiritual ladder? And do I really get that when I do so, I reveal Light in the world? Every time I am put down and others tell me, "You can't make it" or "You won't get there," do I throw in the towel, or do I see it as an opportunity and push forward?

There is a simple kabbalistic story, which reminds us that in every difficulty is a gift.

There once was a man who was beloved and trusted by the king, and the king's advisors were very jealous of this friend. When the king had to leave on a journey, he asked only his trusted friend to watch over the palace. While the king was away, the jealous advisors spread malicious stories about this man and had him flogged for treason. When the king returned and found his beloved friend bleeding and beaten, he demanded to know, "What happened? Who did this to you?"

The man replied, "After you left, your advisors, who are jealous of me, spread lies about me and whipped me for treason."

"How many times did they whip you?" asked the king.

"Thirty-six times," replied the man.

And with that, the king took out thirty-six gold coins and gave them to his dear friend; one gold coin for each time the whip damaged his form. When the man returned home, he cried. His wife was confused and asked, "Why do you cry now?"

The man replied, "I wish they had beaten me more."

God forbid, we should take the metaphor literally, but the

story does ask us to look at our difficulties from a different perspective, and to appreciate them for what they truly are—opportunities to reveal more of who we are in this world.

Whatever is happening in our lives is meant to bring us to the next level. The consciousness that can guide us through challenging times is: I do not know why I have to take this path, but I do know this road will lead me to a better place in the end.

If we want to change something in the physical world, we need to make an effort spiritually, and be willing to face the challenges.

YOU CAN MAKE MIRACLES

Revealed in the 13th century, the *Zohar* (Hebrew for "Splendor" or "Radiance") is a spiritual text that explains the secrets of the Bible, the universe, and the mysteries of life. In the portion of Beshalach, the *Zohar* explains that God gave the 72 Names of God to Moses as a means to split the Red Sea. The 72 Names of God are not "names" in the ordinary sense; they are a metaphysical instrument for connecting to the infinite spiritual current that flows throughout reality. God gave this technology to Moses to share with all people of the world.

כהת	אכא	ללה	מהש	עלם	סיט	ילי	והו
הקם	הרי	מבה	יזל	ההע	לאו	אלד	הזי
וחו	מלה	ייי	נלך	פהל	לוו	כלי	לאו
ושר	לכב	אום	ריי	שאה	ירת	האא	נתה
ייז	רהע	וזעם	אני	מנד	כוק	להח	יוו
מיה	עשל	ערי	סאל	ילה	וול	מיכ	ההה
פוי	מבה	נית	ננא	עמם	הוש	דני	והו
מוי	ענו	יהה	ומב	מצר	הרח	ייל	נמם
מום	היי	יבם	ראה	ובו	איע	מנק	דמב

When the Israelites faced the sea in front of them, and the Egyptian army was fast approaching from the rear, they cried out to God to save them. God's response to the Israelites was, "Why are you calling out to me?" The *Zohar* explains that God was telling the people that they had the power to escape from peril on their own. When God told the Israelites to jump into the sea, it was an encoded message that certainty is the secret for activating the power of the 72 Names of God.

Just before the Pharaoh reached the Israelites, the Red Sea parted and the Israelites crossed over to freedom. The *Zohar* explains that it was not God who parted the sea; it was Moses using the 72 Names of God to engineer this amazing feat. However, before the waters rose to the sky and parted, a physical action was required to activate the power of the 72 Names of God. This is the secret meaning behind God's response, "Go jump in the water." The Israelites demonstrated total certainty in the 72 Names of God by physically walking into the sea with the conviction of a positive outcome.

Naturally, their first instincts were fear and doubt. But when Moses reminded them of the 72 Names of God, they meditated upon them, employing all their mental powers to arouse breathtaking spiritual forces. The waters became completely still when the Israelites conquered their doubts and waded into the sea, neck-deep. Even as the water reached their nostrils, they maintained complete certainty—and the waters parted, giving them passage to freedom.

The 72 Names of God were given at the time and place when a miracle was sorely needed, so that we can draw from the same power and use it when we need it today. But it is not enough to simply use the 72 Names of God; it also means we have to be willing to risk, to sacrifice, to give something up in its place—otherwise the instrument does not work. The 72 Names of God only work with a personal sacrifice of ego.

For instance, there might be a situation in which we must be willing to do what we know is the right thing, even if it means we will not be loved or accepted by everyone when we do it. Sacrifice might also mean that we need to withhold our opinion and not say negative things about other people. Without this kind of effort on our part, the 72 Names of God cannot empower things to happen.

To take control of our lives, to engineer miracles where and when we need them most, we must have certainty in our ability to affect matter. God created this world for humanity to achieve mastery over it with our consciousness. We have to know deep down that we can make anything happen, and we have to act with this knowing. When we combine this consciousness with the divine tool of the 72 Names of God, we can make miracles happen.

REMEMBER YOUR GREATEST ENEMY IS WITHIN

We learn that Jacob feared his brother Esau, for it is said: "Please deliver me from the hand of my brother, from the hand of Esau, for I fear him, that he may come and attack me, the mothers with the children." (Genesis 32:11)

How can it be that such a righteous soul, Jacob, one of the patriarchs—who became the spiritual channel of Central Column for the whole world could harbor such fear of his brother? After all, did Jacob not know that Light prevails over darkness?

There is such an important secret here: Esau was the essence and personification of ego. Jacob did not fear the physicality of his brother; Jacob was afraid of his own ego. Even at his elevated spiritual level, Jacob knew that if he believed himself to be the message rather than the messenger, to be the Light rather than a conduit, he would lose the battle against the ultimate destructive force—the ego, also known as the Opponent and the Desire to Receive for the Self Alone. For Jacob it was clear that he was engaged in a battle of consciousness, and his true strength was his ability to be a channel for the Light of the Creator.

Part of our spiritual work is to cultivate a healthy fear of our own ego every day. This is what Jacob was worried about. He was afraid his ego would create a spiritual blindness and that he would not be consciously present when he was needed to be, and therefore he would lose the battle.

Jacob reminds us that we always need to be on the lookout for what our ego wants us to do. There is only one block in every person's life—a block that is not outside of us; it is our ego from within. When we stop listening to the voice that tells us to only consider our own needs and agendas, then we will begin to taste the sweetness of our soul's potential.

DECLINE BRIBES OF THE SOUL

"Do not accept a bribe, for a bribe blinds those who see."
—Exodus 23:8

We may believe there are no opportunities for bribes in our lives. But what the Bible is referring to here is not a physical payment, it is the permission we give ourselves on a daily basis to be bribed by the energy of a momentary thrill. When we get energy from thoughts and interactions, when we sneak out and do things that we know are wrong for us, and for others, it feeds us in the moment. Appearances can bribe us. For example, when physical things stir our immediate desire, we then seek to fulfill it. These are bribes that place a cover on our soul, and we lose our ability to see and distinguish truth from fiction.

We may be in a good relationship, and then we meet an attractive person. Our primitive desire can allow us to think about all the ways this person could make us feel good. And the little voice inside says this is no big deal, it is just a harmless flirtation. Or we may be paying off a debt, or saving money for school, and along the way our desire is roused for a new gadget, and we say we will begin to save again tomorrow... it is just this one thing, and on and on. This is the bribing of our soul.

Whatever feeds our ego, our Desire to Receive for the Self Alone, actually starves our soul because the covering disrupts our soul's connection to the Light. It impairs our ability to see and receive enjoyment from those things that really do serve us long term. When we accept energetic bribes, we create more curtains that blind us from the truth and from ourselves.

THE ANSWER SHOULD BE SIMPLE

The Bible tells us about a man named Naaman, the chief military officer to a king who was stricken with leprosy. Naaman was advised to go to the prophet Elisha who would inform him of a cure for the king. (2 Kings 5) When Naaman arrived to meet Elisha, he was greeted not by the prophet himself but by one of Elisha's messengers. The messenger described a simple remedy: "The king should immerse himself in the Jordan River." The messenger was referring to the kabbalistic practice of *Mikveh*—spiritual cleansing by submerging in water.

Having received this prescription from Elisha's messenger, Naaman was angry. He had wanted to receive information directly from the prophet, and he thought that Elisha was disrespectful to his position as a messenger of the king. Naaman had traveled such a long distance to see the great prophet. He expected more. In short, the counsel Naaman sought on behalf of the king came in a completely different package than he had expected.

We too can be disappointed. If our ego is not stroked, we can refuse to see the answer we seek is right in front of us. We can miss it because it did not come with the pomp and circumstance we anticipated or because the answer can seem too simple. Either way, it is important that we remember: Light and truth are simple.

We all spend our lives "seeking" the truth in one form or another. Sadly, though, we would prefer to "seek" the truth than "find" it because finding it might mean that we have to do something about it. Spiritually speaking, the truth is always right there in front of us but we often do not accept it because we do not like how it is wrapped. If we can remain open, we will be able to find the solution we are looking for.

UNDERSTAND BLESSINGS AND CURSES

What does it really mean to be blessed or cursed?

We often fall into the illusion that being blessed means getting what we want or having the best of the fruitfulness of this world. Yet sometimes, we can get what we think we want, and later it becomes a curse or a burden that we must bear. For some people, having material wealth can be a curse because they are surrounded by abundance yet still feel empty and lost. On the other hand, there are individuals who do not have much in the way of possessions, and yet they live a full happy life.

Of course, when the Bible speaks about curses and blessings, it is not referring to physical abundance but to a level of consciousness.

The secret we learn in Kabbalah is that essentially being blessed or cursed is a capacity for vision or a lack of it. A blessing is having the ability to see beyond the present moment and understand where the road we are on can take us. Being blessed is when we feel connected to a higher purpose for our being, understand that our difficulties are gifts, and are able to see why we need to tackle them.

A curse is a lack of vision of something beyond ourselves, a lack of awareness that everything happens to bring us to a higher spiritual level. We have blinders on, and our limited sight holds us back from connecting to, and living with, the knowledge and certainty that there is a creative force, a spiritual system, and a bigger picture at play in our destiny.

Whenever we look at another human being and are jealous of what they have, it is our own envy that saps our Light, leaving us feeling empty.

The idea is simple yet profound, if we take the time to think about it. The punishment for our anger is the anger itself. The curse of our jealousy is jealousy itself. It is our limited consciousness that keeps us locked in, unable to see the joy and experience the good that is around us. In effect, we lose twice. We lose because we want what we cannot have, and the anger or envy that fills our viewfinder blocks us from really seeing and enjoying all that we do have.

If we can really understand this concept, remember it, and bring it into our lives, then we will have the beginning of a completely new view of life—which is a true blessing!

WHAT YOU SAY CREATES YOUR FUTURE

Spiritually, we understand that our words are more than just talk. Kabbalah teaches us that angels take the vibrations of our thoughts, words, and actions to chambers in the Upper Worlds.

They transfer whatever comes out of our mouths and manifest that energy. Like it or not, and believe it or not, our words have power, and we can use that power to do good or to do harm. We can use our words to bring more Light into the world, to create miracles, and to help us manifest our dreams. At the same time, we can use our words to speak ill of others, to bring people down, and add to the darkness in the world. When we become truly cognizant of this aspect of our reality, we will speak and act differently. We would never say words like "Drop dead!" in moments of anger, if we knew there was an angel prepared with a sword to hurt someone we love. We would be mindful not to activate such energy by saying things we do not really mean.

The *Zohar* tells us that our lives are not counted by years but by words. When we have used up our allotted words then our time is up. However, there is a beautiful condition: Words that we use to reveal Light, words of prayer, words of human dignity and tolerance, are not counted. So the more our words are for spiritual and positive purpose, the less words we use up.

ANGELS CAN BE PROVEN BY YOU

Each and every human being has the support and guidance of one primary angel for an entire lifetime—a guardian angel, if you will. Every time we reincarnate, we complete a part of our soul's work. Therefore, in each life, because our job is distinct, we need a different angel each time to support us in our spiritual work.

Rav Isaac Luria (the Ari) teaches ways we can call on our angel guide for help. One way is to go into meditation, to find this angel through the practice of relaxation. Here is how to do it:

> Choose a word or a person's name that resonates with you and repeat it over and over for a minute or more, or however long it takes to get relaxed and focused. Now visualize and feel that you are walking along a country road. In the distance you see a doorway. The doorway opens from bottom to top like a garage door. Approach the door and begin to open it, and as you do, ask to see the entity that is here to assist you.

> Sometimes you will see one, and sometimes you will not. No need to force it. It will come when it is ready. Just continue to sit in the quiet space, and call upon the angel again and again, for as long as you can without straining.

A MEDITATION TO DEFY GRAVITY

Kabbalists celebrate a holiday known as *Tu B'Shevat,* which some people refer to as the "New Year of The Trees." *Tu B'Shevat* literally means the 15th day of the month of *Shevat.* On this day, there is a cosmic opening for connecting to the natural world of trees and vegetation. When we consider the ways that trees grow, we see that they develop against the force of gravity, against the physical laws of the universe. During this holiday, we can receive the spiritual power to overcome our own gravitational pull—those things that keep our consciousness from elevating. There is a visualization we can use to rise up from negativity, deep inside of us, that might be holding us down.

> Find a quiet place. Sit comfortably on a chair, close your eyes and relax your body. In your mind's eye, walk to a beautiful place in nature, to a forest, or a place in which you feel the purity of the Creator's Light. Visualize the environment around you and see if there is anything in your surroundings with which you really connect.

> Look for something you can focus on, then once your internal gaze is fixed on it, try to understand yourself by connecting to the subject of your attention. You may feel your heart is closed and it may be a stone that captures your interest. Or

maybe it is a leaf that is part of a beautiful big tree. Or maybe you connect to a bird that has some message for you. Whatever it is, open yourself up to the natural forces around you. Use this powerful energy to take a look and understand a different part of yourself.

Remember, this is simply an opportunity to be like the trees and go against our nature so that we can become the people we are truly meant to be.

A MEDITATION TO WELCOME THE SABBATH

There is a kabbalistic precept that is performed on Friday night to usher in the Sabbath: The woman or women of the house light candles, and then make a prayer of blessing on them. This is a deeply meaningful act. Kabbalistically, we learn the female is the vessel that draws Light into the home, and it is the female who manifests all the energy and puts it in its place, helping others grow. Women are the nourishers of the world. Without the vessel, Light cannot be revealed in this world. The Sun needs the Earth to reflect it in order to reveal its radiance; it cannot illuminate in a void.

I am often asked where we should direct our consciousness as we light the candles. I can share with you what I do, and I hope that it is meaningful for you too.

> Before I light the candles, I breathe deeply and relax my body. I visualize the Holy Temple in Jerusalem, and I walk toward it and climb the stairs. I see all the people I love in my mind's eye, and invite them to join me, holding their hands as I continue climbing.
>
> When I come to the Holy Temple, I connect to my *tzadik* (a righteous person to whom I feel connected), and ask him/her to bless all of us,

and to remain with us for the whole Sabbath. I feel the warmth and love coming from the *tzadik*. I look into the eyes of all the people I love, and in my heart tell them how much I love them.

In my mind's eye, I make a circle and bring them closer, as the *tzadik* moves above the circle. I see a white light above the circle that is filled with the love I am sharing. Speaking to every soul in the circle with each candle I light, I meditate to bring them closer and tell them, "*Shabbat Shalom*," expressing my desire to be together with them on the Sabbath.

THE "RIGHT" WAY TO PRAY

I turned to my son, Michael, at one point during an intense *Yom Kippur* prayer and said, "Half the time when I say these prayers in Hebrew or Aramaic, I am not sure I am expressing them accurately because as you know, Hebrew is not my first language. I wonder if I should just not say them at all, and instead speak my own words and try to connect to the Creator in my own way. If I am praying but not saying the words, is there still a connection taking place?"

His answer was so beautiful that I want to share it with everyone. He said, "It does not matter if you pronounce the words right. As long as you desire to reach that place of connection with the Light of the Creator, then even when you say the words wrong, the listening ear that hears your prayers will turn them around and make them right."

We all make mistakes in the way we pray and in the way we think, yet all we are asked to do is pray in humility, with love and desire, and let the Light work out the rest.

RELATIONSHIPS

Relate to Others as a Divine Spark of God

THERE IS POWER IN COMMUNITY

"Let them make for Me a Sanctuary, so that I shall dwell in their midst."

—Exodus 25:8

The *Zohar* tells us that when the Creator asked Moses to direct the people to build a Tabernacle in the wilderness, the message was not only to construct a physical structure but also a metaphysical space through which every generation can connect with the Light. "Make for Me a Sanctuary, so that I shall dwell in their midst," means create a place inside of you, in your heart and soul, that God can fill. Remove the foolishness, the anger, and the negativity. Take out the darkness that separates you from God and from true fulfillment. Erase the depression and the judgment. Get rid of the selfishness, the "I care only about me" way of being. By ridding ourselves of these things, we create space for the Light to reside within us.

As we are all part of God and can each create oneness with the Creator, there remains the question: Why do we need places to come together to connect? Are we not able to connect at home? The answer, as we understand from the *Zohar*, is that the Creator told Moses to create a place where unity could manifest through an exchange of love. A place we can all go to when we are down or depressed, when we are happy or inspired, or even when we simply feel the desire to be with people who care.

On the one hand, yes, we can connect to the Light by ourselves. Each one of us is given a cord of life, and with this thread we can become like the Creator. Yet we have our frailties as humans, and we require other strings, other energy to combine with our own to form oneness. We need a shared place where we are free to say, "Boy, I messed up and please forgive me." Just as we need to create a metaphysical Tabernacle within, we also need to create a physical Tabernacle for all of us.

There is a story about a kabbalist with tremendous energy who walked into a place of worship. As soon as he arrived, he said to a man sitting at the threshold, "I cannot go inside. It's so full of prayer, of people's wishes and tears, there is no space to walk in."

Surprised and confused but well aware of the power and energy of this great kabbalist, the man responded, "Well, isn't that what we want from a place of prayer? Don't we want it to be full of all these things?"

"No," said the kabbalist, "We want it all to go to the Upper Worlds where the Creator can receive it. The reason their prayers do not go up is because the people are crying and praying individually, and not together as one. There is no unity in this place. Therefore, all of this energy is staying here and cannot be released above."

Through this story we learn that our power to make change—to really make a difference and to have our prayers answered—is possible when we are a part of something larger than ourselves. A tabernacle, from within and from without, is a place where we meet others on the same playing field. It is a place where we can look into each other's eyes and love each other. A place where we can say, "I am sorry," and a place where we can say, "You are forgiven."

GROW CLOSER TO THE LIGHT

The great Kabbalist, the Baal Shem Tov or Master of the Good Name, was known to sometimes walk into a place of prayer and greet people with a salutation normally used when addressing someone who has been away for three or more days. One of the men asked, "Teacher, I haven't left the city. I see you every day. Why is it that every time you see me, you always greet me in this way?"

The Baal Shem Tov responded, "While you are praying, where are you? Are you here, in the present, thinking about spiritual things or are you already at work, or on vacation, or planning to run your errands? I address you this way to make you mindful to be here in body and consciousness."

This story reminds us today of what the Baal Shem Tov was teaching his students hundreds of years ago: When we pray, read from a spiritual book, meditate or use any tools of connection to generate energy for ourselves and for the world, we should check our consciousness and see if it has wandered. Am I in tune with the action I am doing right now? Am I meditating on how I can extend myself to others? Am I focused on what the Creator wants of me? Am I being present and kind with the people around me?

When it comes down to it, we are the only ones who can bring about our own evolution. Growing our consciousness is how we move closer to the Light. To rise above the limitations of the physical world that tries to drag us down, we need to choose to be aware, to be present, so that we do not miss the opportunities before us to share, to learn, and to transform.

By just going along our way while asleep in our life, we are doing what our ego wants, creating a circuitry that is not connected to the Light, thereby diminishing the spiritual Light that guides us. Then it becomes more and more difficult for us to recognize what is negative and what is positive. God forbid that we should reach a state of consciousness where we cannot recognize negativity.

The Bible often talks about the specific restrictions that exist for the *Kohen haGadol*. The *Kohen haGadol* is the High Priest and is a representative of the path of the Creator. I believe each of us is like a *Kohen* (priest). We are all God's people. Each human being has been imbued with a spark of the Creator. Therefore, we can all be like the priest—a channel for someone who needs us. We can be a voice of compassion for one who needs support, we can provide wisdom to a friend who needs guidance, and we can care for someone who needs to feel loved.

LIVING BY ROTE SUFFOCATES OUR LIGHT

The Bible tells us that when the Holy Temple was part of everyday life, there were certain manners and behaviors that were part of a required ritual. Though it was centuries ago, we know the Bible does not give us this knowledge as a history lesson; spiritually, there are things we can understand from it today.

It is explained that those who came to make a sacrifice in the Temple would enter through one door and leave through a different one. Now this minor nuance may seem insignificant or even senseless. Why were the people not able to go out the way they had entered? Why build a different doorway?

Every action associated with the practices of the Holy Temple had a reason. By entering through one door and exiting through another door, the change of route created a different energy, which kept the act of sacrifice from becoming routine.

In human nature, we all too often lose sight of the significance of our daily journey. We forget about, or take for granted, the importance of our relationships. We miss seeing the splendor that is all around us because we are so focused on ourselves. Life becomes something expected and mundane. Our view becomes limited, and we stop seeing all that we receive from the universe. We forget about the endless, renewable spiritual resource we have at our fingertips. We cannot see that it is a beautiful world.

Of course, things happen. But no matter what is happening, every day we live is a miracle. From the moment we breathe air into our lungs, we are given another opportunity to awaken our consciousness to the things that are significant. Each day is another chance to make the people in our lives important. When we see the beauty in something, we actually give it life, and we reveal Light, just like Adam who gave life to the animals simply by naming their species. The Light that we manifest by simple actions of human dignity accumulates Light in our spiritual basket.

Just as the people in the Temple came in one door and left through another, when we leave this world, hopefully we will leave different then when we came in, with all of the Light that we revealed because we existed. What will remain is the basket of energy that we have created because we sacrificed what is rote, and we chose to be awake and aware of the goodness in others and in the universe.

PRACTICE DIFFERENT KINDS OF FORGIVENESS

"If I cannot forgive myself
For all the blunders
I have made
Over the years,
Then how can I proceed?
How can I ever
Dream perfection-dreams?
Move, I must, forward.
Fly, I must, upward,
Dive, I must inward,
To be once more
What I truly am
And shall forever remain."
—Sri Chimnoy, *My Christmas-New Year-Vacation Aspiration-Prayers, Part 21*

There are three types of forgiveness:

- One kind is the forgiveness that we ask from the Creator for the things we have done to damage our connection with Him. We ask for the guidance to keep us from going back to that same consciousness, and for the help to fill ourselves with energy so that we do not need to go there again.

- The second kind of forgiveness is that which we ask from others for the harm we have caused them. We need to find the place within us where we can change our attitude toward those we hurt by uncovering the ego that created the separation between us. It is important to ask forgiveness not only from those we know will forgive us but especially from those who might not.

- The third, and most important kind of forgiveness, is the forgiveness we ask of ourselves. All of us have a life story that shaped who we are. Some of us have had difficult childhoods; some of us have had difficult adulthoods. No matter the circumstance, those are the things for which we need to forgive ourselves. The reason we go through the trials we do is because they are a way of teaching us, challenging us, and pushing us forward to become who we are meant to be. We do not always see it this way. As human beings, we were created predisposed to see the negative, and yet we were also created with the ability to change that.

There is a simple ritual I learned that can help us alter our consciousness.

If you will, take a piece of paper and write down all the things in your nature that you feel bad about; the things you feel are holding you back. Put the letter into an envelope and burn it!

Literally. (Please do so in a safe way and in a safe place, where the fire will remain contained.)

Allow yourself, from tomorrow on, to not look backward and to only go forward. Tell yourself, "I am not ashamed of who I am. God created me with my Light so I can share with others. The level of my Light is not yet known to me but it is increasing because I am committed to my spiritual path."

There is a story from Rav Israel of Salanta, who noticed a light coming from the shoemaker's shop while walking home late one night. He walked in and saw the shoemaker still hard at work. The candle that was lighting his way was flickering at its end. Rav Israel asked the shoemaker, "Why must you work so late?"

And the shoemaker replied, "As long as the light is still burning, I can still do more, I can still fix more."

As long as the Light of our soul is still burning inside of us, we can still change and connect to the Creator.

MAKE ROOM FOR GOD

Let us face it. We all judge. We take a look at people, and we somehow make ourselves more by making others less. We do this by telling ourselves they do things we would never do. Yet if we lived the same way they do, if we went through what they went through, we might be a lot like them.

The problem with judgment is that it fills us up, and then we have no place for love. We get so full of ourselves—who we think we are, what we believe we are entitled to—that there is no space for others, and, more importantly, there is no space for God.

Spiritual work, as explained by the kabbalists, is the work of developing ourselves to become like the Creator. When we behave as the Light does, we actually bring Light into our being. Rav Ashlag explains that this understanding comes from the spiritual concept called Similarity of Form:

> *"Indeed a closeness between spiritual bodies is a matter of Similarity of Form, just as love is a similarity of form and opinions, while hate is the opposite. Consequently, the moment you cancel the Desire to Receive within you, you bring your spiritual body closer to His [the Creator's] Essence because you are totally in the aspect of sharing with others, which is the equivalent of giving pleasure to*

your Maker. This is the intention you want to fulfill so that you will be prepared for the ultimate purpose of Creation."
—*On World Peace,* Chapter 2, Cleaving, pg. 114, Rav Ashlag

When we are in affinity with the Creator, we can connect to His Essence. God sees all of us with our imperfections, and yet continues with infinite mercy and compassion to put breath and life in us.

By opening up our hearts to care, rather than our minds to judge, we expand our capacity for Light. I have a favorite saying that has been attributed to many different authors; nonetheless for me it is simply a wonderful reminder: "There is so much good in the worst of us and so much bad in the best of us that it ill behooves any of us to find fault with the rest of us."

WE ONLY HAVE A SNAPSHOT IN TIME

A student of spirituality approached his teacher and said, "I don't think I can stay on this path any longer. I have so many questions that are unanswered, so much that I don't understand. I think this is simply not for me."

The teacher calmly responded, "Did these questions come to you before or after you decided this was not for you?"

When we want to quit something or when we want to do something, we can create within our mind situations to support the case we want to build. This is also true of our relationships with people.

Armed with our preconceptions, we close the door of our heart instead of leaving it open for others to walk through. We create what, at The Kabbalah Centre, is known as "a movie" that serves our ideas and beliefs. This can keep us from seeing the beauty that is around us; it can rob us of relationships and joy.

The Bible tells us that Moses asked God, "Please show me Your glory." And God said, "You shall see My back, but My face shall not be seen." (Exodus 33:23) Here the Creator is reminding Moses, and all of us, that we do not see the whole picture. The spiritual system was created this way for a reason: So we can choose to see beyond and rise above the movies in our heads.

As we go deeper into our spiritual work, remember that if we want to connect to the face of the Creator, we should come with questions rather than answers; prepare ourselves for new experiences, and view ourselves and our perspective as infinitesimal with respect to the world of the Light. The following idea is commonly attributed to Socrates, "The more I know, the more I understand how little I know." Also, the Rav would always say, "If we want to become somebody, then first we have to understand that we are nobody."

Being in awe of all that exists beyond our understanding, and having an appreciation of the Creator's presence in our lives, can help us override our stock answers with new questions. Paradoxically, achieving this level of humility unhinges the ego from our view and allows us to experience a bigger picture.

LOVE IS ONENESS

Kabbalah uses a system of numerology, where each letter of the Hebrew alphabet is assigned a numerical value. This is a way to assist us in expanding our understanding of the language. For example, the word *ahava*, which means "love," has the numerical value of 13, as does the word *echad*, which means "one."

Why is this significant?

We can experience the true oneness of love from the Creator who gives us life. The same Divine Light affords us the free will to complete the process of the body that was created for our soul at this juncture in time. Just as the Light requires a vessel with which to share, we also need someone with whom to share our love.

When love, *ahava* (13) and one, *echad* (13) are combined, they equal 26. Twenty-six is also the numerical value of the Tetragrammaton יְהֹוָה —the four-letter Name of God, and the highest level of spirituality. We reach the ultimate connection to the Light of the Creator when two become one, united by love.

SATISFY YOUR DEEPEST DESIRES

To find what is eluding us, we can begin by looking at how we tie ourselves to temporary satisfactions instead of life's true and lasting gifts. We can become slaves to relationships, money, work, and sometimes even drugs and alcohol. Often, these preoccupations become our escape routes from real life and transformation, allowing us to hide behind whatever we think we want to be when we are trying to be something we are not.

Kabbalistically speaking, to be a slave to anything is to deny the fact that we are part of the Creator. We each have the ability to do what we want with our physical body, whether it is negative or positive. (All of us will do negative things; there is no question about that.) The point is to understand that the fulfillment we seek in this world lies in the spiritual work of overpowering the consciousness that life is "only about me."

If we spend our days chasing things that do not satisfy our soul's deepest desires for fulfillment, we will eventually feel empty and joyless. If we work only to serve the body, we will starve this all-important aspect of our being. This does not mean we need to renounce the physical world but rather to transcend its control over us. Ultimately, we discover that deep, lasting happiness can come only when our souls are fed—and the food that satisfies the soul comes to us when we manage to become proactive beings of sharing.

PARENT, KNOW THYSELF

I have two incredible daughters from my first marriage; one has blessed me with five grandchildren and the other with two grandchildren. I was very young when my girls were born and did not have the time, patience or ability to give them as much attention as I would have liked. Still, they always knew that I love them.

The Rav and I raised our two sons in Israel. We were just beginning to organize our lives. We knew we wanted to create a lasting effect on humanity in a spiritual way and believed that Kabbalah was the way to do so. We were highly controversial back then, so we had few family members around us—no students, no Centre activities, and little money. Yet our scant means became one of our biggest blessings. As we were pretty much alone we had more time to be with our children. We would spend each night singing songs together. Sometimes the Rav would tell us the story about his favorite fictional horse Silver, and about the imaginary farm where he rode him. Those were the very best years of our lives.

Today, with the fast pace of life, most people do not have the luxury of being with their family as much as we were. Nevertheless, I believe that finding even an hour a day to tell your children a story, and give yourself to them completely, is possible and important. It does wonders for them and for you.

Parenting, like life, does not come with a user's manual. Knowing what, when, and how much to do for our children is a constant challenge and universal quest. Here are a few things I have learned over the years:

- Parenting is measured little by what we tell our children, some by what we do for our children, and mostly by who we are.

- The most valuable things we give our children are our time and our example. By example, I mean that we behave the way we wish our children to behave. If we sit down every evening to unwind with a few drinks, then we should not be surprised and concerned if our children drink or use drugs. Whatever we want for and from our children, we must first demand of ourselves.

- For children to be safe and well, they need more than food and shelter for their body; they need to feed and protect their soul. Spirituality is not only something to be taught, it is something to be practiced. Primarily, our role as parents is to give our children the very best we have of ourselves, not of our things. Our soul, our heart, and the example of our choices are what exemplify the very best of us.

- While children need energy and guidance to develop a sense of themselves and their world, they also require some healthy space to express their own thoughts and learn from their own mistakes.

- If a child sees or feels the presence of something scary, do not shrink their imagination by saying there is no such thing as a boogeyman. Instead, allow them to discover the metaphysical world in a safe way by teaching them that there are good angels who watch over all of us, and that sometimes they frighten us too because we do not know what they are. Make up a little prayer with your children to welcome these wonderful forces into their life. There are beautiful prayers in every language to teach children. By doing this, you guide them to become attuned with the cosmic energies that exist around us.

- There is an excellent exercise that you can do with your child at night while he or she is asleep. Run your hands about two or three inches above your child's body from head to toe, as you choose a color you think he or she might need. For instance, if your child has temper tantrums, choose a blue or a green, both soothing colors, and go over their body, sending this energy into them. You will be surprised how much of a difference this can make to your child's well-being. It is far more powerful to respond to problems on a metaphysical level than on a physical one. Moreover, children under the age of twelve function in alpha state all the time, and are much more capable of being influenced by consciousness-raising techniques.

It is terribly sad when parents lose contact and connection with the most precious gift the Creator has given them—their children. Loving and nurturing our young is not our responsibility to them; it is a gift for us.

Becoming the kind of person our children respect and wish to emulate is not easy work but it is loving work. In truth, it is our spiritual work. It demands being true to ourselves, for children can see in a minute what is real and what is not.

Indeed, the most powerful parenting tool we have is the ability to look inside ourselves and decide if we are really the person we want to be, and if we really do share ourselves and our love with those around us.

REVEAL YOUR GREATNESS

The *Book of Joshua* tells an enlightening story about a prostitute named Rahab who protected Pinchas and Caleb from discovery, and probable death, by hiding them on her roof. In return, Rahab asked that she and her family would be allowed to enter Israel when the Israelites took over Canaan. Rahab was a child when the Israelites were freed from Egypt. She had learned about the miracles that God had performed to protect the people. She was certain that just such a miracle would take place again, and that they would defeat Jericho and conquer Canaan.

Her certainty in the Light, as well as the risk she took, gave Rahab a way into a land that even Moses himself was not allowed to enter. Rahab was a prostitute and yet she was secured redemption for her whole family as a result of this one act.

For us, the lesson is that we can never decide on a person's spiritual value or worth, nor can we determine a person's future greatness by their present position. We can never judge what someone is capable of spiritually. Sometimes it takes only one act of kindness and generosity to transform a lifetime of negativity.

Transforming our Desire to Receive for the Self Alone into a Desire to Share with Others is where our greatness is revealed. It can take a lifetime or a moment to achieve it.

With one act of complete selflessness, Rahab shifted the destiny for her entire family. What will be your act?

FEEL THE PAIN OF OTHERS

Some people believe spirituality means protecting ourselves from the world at large so that we can stay holy and pure, isolating ourselves with scripture, and keeping ourselves from the negativity of the world. But kabbalistically, spiritual work is about engaging with the world and being involved with people. The more work we do with and for others—not separate from them—the higher we evolve.

Furthermore, the greater the effort we make to share and become involved in others' lives, the greater the blessings we receive back into our own life. There is an enlightening lesson about 17th century kabbalist and storyteller, the Maggid of Mezrich, considered to be one of the most learned sages of his time. His wife prodded him to seek a meeting with the Baal Shem Tov, believed to be the most enlightened holy soul of his generation. Despite the Maggid's resistance, his wife finally wore him down and he conceded to travel during the freezing cold Russian winter to find the Baal Shem Tov.

After a long and difficult journey, the Maggid arrived at the house of the sage. That evening at dinner, the Baal Shem Tov stated, "Once when I was traveling, we came to the middle of the forest and there was no hay for the horse until someone came along and offered us some hay."

Naturally, the Maggid was confused. He tried to make sense of what the master had said because sometimes it is difficult to understand the message underlying the words of a spiritual teacher. But to no avail. The next day the Maggid returned, and the Baal Shem Tov again spoke about his horse. "Once when I was traveling under the scorching sun, and there was no drink for the horse, a man suddenly appeared carrying water buckets."

The Maggid understood from these two messages that there is Divine assistance when we need it, and with that simple lesson, he planned to return home.

Before his departure, the Maggid stopped to say goodbye to the great master. At that moment, the Baal Shem took out the *Kitvei Ha'Ari* or *Writings of the Ari*, and opened to a passage. He passed the book to the Maggid and said, "Teach me what this is saying." The Maggid explained the lesson clearly and perfectly. The Baal Shem Tov then read the same passage, but when he read, the angels whose names were discussed in the passage, appeared. The Baal Shem Tov turned to the Maggid and said, "You see, it's not what you know, it's what you feel. You understand the 'body' of the hidden Torah. But you have not penetrated its 'soul.'"

We can isolate ourselves and become the brightest scholars, citing spiritual verses, and explaining them with our mind's understanding. But this is not what the work of revealing the Light of the Creator is all about. To create an internal evolution, we want to awaken our feeling, to push outside of ourselves, and to extend ourselves toward others.

It can be as simple as making one person feel better or more motivated to become involved in his or her own relationship with the Light. Ultimately, it is about opening our heart and feeling the pain of others. This is what spirituality is really all about.

INJECT SHARING INTO YOUR LIFE

I will never forget a news story about a man who stopped to help two women whose car had a flat tire on a remote highway. Minutes after this Good Samaritan got back into his car and started driving, he had a heart attack. The women he had just helped were able to pull the car over, perform CPR, and save his life. There are so many ways to look at this miracle. The bottom line is that as a result of this man's effort to help two strangers, his life was saved. This incredible story reveals the power of being merciful and sharing.

When we are a part of something bigger than ourselves we can actually rise above the things that hold us down: Heaviness, depression, procrastination, anger, and even death. Mercy is our umbilical cord to life. The acts of kindness we do for others activate the universe to produce mercy in return for us.

The *Zohar* explains that Abraham opened the viaduct for mercy in the cosmos with his actions. Abraham was considered the kindest and most generous person to walk this Earth, and he became the chariot of this *Chesed* (Mercy) for all humankind. The path was never easy for him. His tests were many and difficult. Nevertheless, he was a man of action, a doer. The Bible tells us that even when in excruciating physical pain in the heat of the day, Abraham still longed for people to come to his home so he could serve them and perform acts of kindness.

There is so much abundance woven into the fabric of this universe, so much potential for blessings, happiness, love, and transformation, and this energy can be activated with the energy of Abraham. Let us try, in simple ways, to include others in our daily comings and goings and bring kindness into every encounter. Perhaps you can make the effort to hold the door for the person behind you, to smile more in the office, to complete those thank-you cards you have been meaning to write or to go out of your way to listen to a friend. The Light will always provide opportunities if we are open to them.

LIGHT

Rise Above the Darkness to Be the Light

RISE ABOVE THE DARKNESS

In the biblical portion of Vayetze, we are told that Jacob traveled from the most powerfully positive land of Israel to a most negative land called Haran. The journey was long and difficult, and there were many obstacles along the way. (Genesis 28:10) Why did Jacob leave a positive place? Why did he have to endure such hardship? It was in going through this process that he was able to reach his potential. To complete both his physical and spiritual work, he had to leave Israel (positivity) and go to Haran (negativity).

On the road of life, we do not anticipate that our process must have complications, things that get in our way. Essentially, the more difficult the process, the more capable the individual, the stronger the vessel and the higher the individual can climb on the ladder of spirituality. Each of us has been put in the most perfect situation for us to become the brightest Light possible. Every difficulty that we experience is an opportunity for us to climb the next rung. But we need to pay attention to the things around us so that we can grow from them.

When things are going well, all of us, including myself, are very spiritual. But when things seem to be going wrong, everything we know goes out the window. We kick over the bucket. We throw all the notes on the floor. We yell, "Help, help!"

Take a good look at your life; when things are not the way you want them to be, how do you react? How certain are you on your spiritual journey? Do you understand the reason why you are here, and all that you are is your ability to climb that mountain? Life here, on this physical realm, is like Haran. It is a dimension often shrouded in veils of negativity. In a world where chaos—from natural disasters, war, terrorism, and economic instability—is rampant, we may wonder if there is a way to be protected from this negativity. Well, there is, and it is up to us.

Through our positive actions, we have the power to create a spiritual shield that can protect us from negativity that crosses our path. We live in the world of manifestation where the Creator is revealed through our positive deeds. We ask to see God and to feel His presence. But all too often, in our search to see and feel the Creator, we overlook opportunities that are right in front of us—opportunities in the form of someone we can help or a situation in which we can be of service. These are chances we are given to build our Light, to fortify our protective shield, and to give us the strength to know that we are totally capable of rising above what is going on in our lives, no matter how bad things may seem.

CONQUER OPPRESSION

Dehumanizing, terrible things are happening all over our world, and it seems that every day brings a new revolution. This chaos is the universe's way of showing us that our old ways do not work, and that we need to change or stay the same and perish.

What we see today is the long-term effect of lack of consciousness. It is the absence of respect for others and for our planet. It is our selfish behavior that is causing the spiritual and physical global backlash.

Kabbalistically, we can create change by seeing the spark of Light rather than the darkness in everyone and everything with which we interact. This is human dignity, and this is where to begin.

We are starting to see glimpses of this around the world. But for this to happen in a meaningful and lasting way, each one of us needs to take responsibility: To be a force of kindness in every area of our lives. It might seem like we cannot influence world events but when we change these seemingly small and insignificant selfish actions, not only *can* we change the world, we *will* change the world.

THERE IS A LIGHT THAT BINDS
AMID DISASTER

If each incident were a word in the language of the world, what would the world be saying?

It seems from minute to minute there is some new disaster making headlines. We are just recovering from one world-altering, paradigm-shifting event, and another follows. There are revolutions, earthquakes, tsunamis, and animals dying en-mass.

Often in the wake of catastrophic devastation, when the Earth shudders and rips off our masks, we remember who we really are and see our underlying similarities. Out of the rubble of destruction, we find proof that the human spirit is illuminating our way home. I heard a story about a rescue worker in Japan who pulled a woman from a car and did not just give her aid, he gave her a hug as well. That was beyond the call of duty—heart touching heart.

It would be amazing if we could recall the Divine beings we are without the need of difficult circumstances to awaken it within us. Imagine if, at every given moment, we were aware that within each person exists the Light of God. Imagine if we could get to the place in our consciousness where we not only see but also respect that Light and give the person housing it the dignity and space he or she deserves to live freely.

"Everything that exists in our world has a right to exist because it has the Light within it. Therefore we need to understand and to take great care that we do not find faults in any part of Creation, declaring this or that to be superfluous or unnecessary, because this amounts to giving a bad name to He Who created it." Rav Ashlag wrote this in 1922, in an article entitled "World Peace." It was the same year he founded The Kabbalah Centre for the purpose of bringing this awareness to the world. I hope his profound message will inspire our daily thoughts, words, and actions. Let us not wait for another disaster headline to rewrite the story of humanity.

CREATING LIGHT FOR OURSELVES AND THE WORLD

"Mercy and Truth have met,
Righteousness and peace have kissed.
Truth will rise up from the Earth,
And Righteousness looks upon from Heaven.
And the Creator will give goodness
And our land will yield its crops."
—Psalms 85:11-13

The realm of existence that we inhabit on the physical level is what Kabbalah refers to as *Malchut.* The vessel for the Light of the Creator, *Malchut,* has no Light of its own. Our purpose, as we travel through this empty dimension, is to fill it with Light through our effort to generate positivity no matter what the circumstance.

The ancient kabbalists explained that during our time, the Age of Aquarius, the Light would begin to enter the vessel as a matter of course and not from our doing. As the Light from the Upper Dimensions descends to *Malchut,* it will create a pressure that will manifest as challenges and difficulties. This is to give us a chance to make an effort, and in doing so, we become a cause of that revelation.

The reason things will become more difficult as we get closer to this time is because of the polarity that exists in the universe.

Where there is Light, there must be an equal measure of darkness. The greater the revelation of Light, the greater the force of darkness will be to create a balance of free will.

Those of us in the world who seek understanding will come to realize that the reason we are being challenged is because through these challenges we find out who we are and of what we are made. And at the same time, each of us represents a world unto him or herself. While we are a microcosm, we contribute to the macrocosm.

This knowledge can help us to change the world—one person at a time.

WAKING UP

There is a religious practice to bless the food we eat. Yet the Rav always reminded us that the Creator does not need our blessings. The reason we bless the food is to train our mind to be conscious and aware; to help us remember that the Light exists all around us, in every action we do. From the moment we wake in the morning, until we go to sleep at night, life gives us the choice to be robotic or conscious with the people around us, in our work, and as we travel to and from one destination to another.

Sometimes when driving home, the drive itself can become so automatic that you can find yourself home and not remember how you got there. When actions become routine, we can stop operating on a conscious level. Waking up to be conscious of the Creator is part of our soul's process of evolution.

THERE IS AN ALTERNATIVE TO PAIN AND SUFFERING – PART 1

The *Zohar*, written more than 2000 years ago, described the 21st century as a period where two aspects of consciousness would prevail: *Oy* (Woe) and *Ashrei* (Blessed).

Oy refers to the mindset of people who experience this world without spirituality and who do not understand the need for a change in consciousness. *Ashrei* refers to the consciousness of people who experience this world as a spiritual place, who take responsibility for what they contribute to the collective, and who work hard to transform their nature to practice greater love and tolerance. In a consciousness of *Ashrei*, we as human beings understand that we have the inherent ability to evolve ourselves. Rav Ashlag calls this ability the "Governance of Heaven" and describes it as follows:

> *"The Creator has bestowed wisdom and governance upon humans and has enabled them to take the said law of evolution under their own authority and governance, and in doing so allows one to greatly accelerate the process of evolution, according to his will and in complete freedom and independence, with respect to the limitation and time."*
> —*On World Peace*, Rav Ashlag, Governance of Heaven and Governance of the Earth

Referring to this time period, the Creator said, "I will refine them as silver is refined, and will try them as gold is tried." (Zachariah 13:9) The *Zohar* explains this to mean that during this time, to awaken humanity to the consciousness of the Light of the Creator, the universe will clean us the same way a carpet is beaten to shake out all the dust and dirt from its fibers. Those with *Oy* consciousness will experience the beating, and those with *Ashrei* consciousness will experience the cleaning.

When "bad" things happen, they are not actually bad, they are meant to bring us to a better way of doing things. As we know, the Light does not come from Light, it comes from darkness. Through the darkness, through the sludge, through the dirt, we can reach the heights of our spirituality. People with Ashrei consciousness experience challenges in this way.

There is a spiritual understanding that in this physical world we are meant to do this work ourselves, and if we do not, the universe will do it for us. The Creator will send us a little nudge. If we miss it, we will get a heavier nudge. If this still does not do the trick, we will get that real big push. This is what is happening in the world right now. We have been warned over and over again. We need to begin seeing how we are destroying the things around us. And we need to stop.

The *Zohar* tells us that humanity has the capacity to change the trajectory of the state of the world. Through our transformation in consciousness and our actions, we can create a reality of *Ashrei* for us all.

THERE IS AN ALTERNATIVE TO PAIN AND SUFFERING – PART 2

"For one human being to love another human being:
That is perhaps the most difficult task that has been given to us,
The ultimate, the final problem and proof,
The work for which all other work is merely preparation."
—*The Selected Poetry of Rainer Maria Rilke*, Rainer Maria Rilke

The gap between cause and effect is shrinking as never before in history. In the past, we were given time between action and effect to repent and change our ways. Now things happen in an instant. It is like sticking your finger in an electric socket—the shock is sudden.

What are we to do? To start, each day we can ask ourselves, "What is it that I can do today that I did not do yesterday? What is it that I can change? Where have I fallen? What is it that I can do to create unity?"

If we look for massive change every day, we will not find it. But when we look for the small things to change—the way we interact with others; the times we give a smile instead of a judgment—we create a shift and bring the whole world along with us.

It does not matter what spiritual path we follow, be it Judaism, Christianity, Buddhism or Islam. All our teachers embodied the same message, which was a signal for life's greatest purpose. Buddha said, "Consider others as yourself." Jesus said, "Love thy neighbor as thyself." Mohammed said, "That which you want for yourself, seek for mankind." Hillel said, "That which is odious to you, do not do to others."

One way to practice this Golden Rule is to take it upon ourselves to help others with their problems as if they are our own. It is so easy to think, "This issue doesn't affect me," but in the eyes of God, we are one. This is why it is important to come together every day through prayer, to garner ourselves with a new consciousness, one that does not only think of our own pain and problems, but also about the pain and problems of others as well. We are all connected, and we all affect each other. By helping others with their problems, we truly help ourselves. To create this revolution in consciousness, we need to make awareness a lifestyle.

CREATING BLESSINGS FOR US AND THE WORLD

We can look at what is going on around the world and think: "I see what's happening but what does it have to do with me? What can I do about it?" On the other hand, we can ask ourselves these questions instead: "What I can do to make sure that my own channel is clear? How am I interacting with others? Am I open to accepting criticism in the right way and growing from it? Am I looking to see things around me that I can improve? Am I motivating the people around me for good?"

If we can wake up in the morning and set our intention to connect with our own spirituality, making sure that we do not bring more negativity into this world, then this consciousness can spread to others around us, and from them outwards. Multiply this positive consciousness, and together we will alter the way the world looks. This is what we can do about it!

Within every human being there are two forces: There is the soft voice of the Light inside of us that nudges us and says: "Help your friend. Go out of your way to make that phone call." And then there is another much louder voice, the Desire to Receive for the Self Alone, which says: "Take a little extra for yourself; Cheat your partner, he won't know the difference." Every day, we can choose which force to listen to. Our choices make a difference in the health of this world.

Every day, let us ask ourselves again: "What's it all about? Is it about the few moments of my selfish pleasure, or is it about being victorious in bringing the world well-being? Will we do things that serve only ourselves or will we do things that benefit others as well?"

May we all develop a true desire that will result in blessings for each of us, and for the world.

ATTAIN *Binah*CONSCIOUSNESS

Binah is the spiritual level of Understanding on the Kabbalistic Tree of Life. It is a pure reflection of the Light of Wisdom, which is at the level of *Chochmah*.

Angels are on the level of *Binah* and have the ability to understand exactly what the Light of the Creator is asking them to do. Every angel has a job, which it performs completely and without hesitation.

On the other hand, we, on the level of *Malchut*, are faced with the illusion of time, space, and the physicality of this world. These limitations present us with the free will to make choices, deciding for ourselves what we are meant to do, not because we are told to do it.

For those of us on a spiritual path, seeking to stay in alignment with the Lightforce of the Creator, knowing what to do and when do it is a constant challenge. We ask for the guidance that will allow us to open the right door and make the right choice.

This choice was something Jonah faced at the age of 13. Jonah was told by the Creator to go to the town of Nineveh and bring the people closer to God. Nineveh was a notorious town filled with negative people, and Jonah did not understand how he could help them change their ways.

Eventually through a process, which involved being swallowed by a whale for three days, Jonah was finally ready to accept responsibility for his destiny.

The *Zohar* teaches us that this process of choice exists for all of us. Each one of us has a destiny to fulfill. And spiritually, we know that the right choice always comes down to sharing Light beyond our own lives. Most of us wish for ourselves, our families, and the people close to us to have a life that is calm and without negativity. But oftentimes we are called to awaken this type of care for those outside of our circles, to do something that benefits the greater collective, as Jonah was called to do.

Jonah was swallowed by the whale because he needed to get to a difficult place where he would not be heard or supported, and awaken care for the people around him anyway. When we go to these difficult places, with effort and care we can turn on the Light for ourselves and for others. That is our free will as humanity, and in choosing it we become like the angels accessing *Binah*.

BE A CHILD OF GOD

The *Zohar* reveals many beautiful things to assist us in understanding our relationship with the Creator. One such discussion relates the difference between being a servant of God and a child of God. In one instance, the *Zohar* states that the Creator says, "The people of Israel are my servants." (Leviticus 25:55) Yet, in another place, the Creator says, "These are my children." (Isaiah 63:8) The *Zohar* explains these two distinctions are connected to the different levels of consciousness of the Israelites at different times.

In one circumstance, the *Zohar* says that to be a servant of God is to be someone who performs his duty because it is what he was told to do; he does it robotically as if he had no choice.

On the other hand, a child of God is someone whose consciousness leads him to do things because he sees the bigger picture, not because of what is expected of him. He knows who he is and who he was born to be. He perceives himself to be a child of the Creator, and is aware of the Creator within him. A child of God is a person who knows he or she will become more connected to the Lightforce of God by doing certain actions. Essentially, as a servant, we are an effect of the master; as a child, we are made from the same essence as our parent, and we live that reality from a place of love, not obligation.

Our work is to choose the path of the Creator because it is something we want, not because it is what we are supposed to do. Each and every time we desire and choose to behave according to the spiritual laws the Creator has set out for us, we become the writers of our own destiny. This is why we, at The Kabbalah Centre, believe that there is no coercion in spirituality, for it would take away our ability to be the cause, to decide for ourselves.

In the *Zohar* (Behar 9:58-62), we find a story that reveals a choice that changed a man's destiny. Rav Chiya and Rav Yosi, two students of Rav Shimon bar Yochai, were walking in the desert. They observed two other men traveling, when a third man approached. The third man said that he was starving and asked if the men could spare some food or drink. One of the men answered, "I only have enough to complete my journey. I have no food to spare."

The other man said, "I will share my food and water as I am well now and do not need it as much as he does."

Still observing, the two students of Rav Shimon noticed that the man who shared his food was becoming weaker and weaker in time. Rav Yosi said to Rav Chiya, "We must help him and give him food."

Rav Chiya said, "I believe there is a miracle meant to happen here. Let us first observe and not interfere with the opportunity the Creator has presented this man." Exhausted, hungry and thirsty, the weary traveler lay down to rest by a rock, under a small patch of shade.

The man, who had held onto his food, said, "I told you to keep your food and drink, I cannot wait. I will continue on my way."

While asleep at the rock, a rattlesnake approached him. Rav Yosi said again, "We must help," when just then, a much larger snake appeared, ate the first snake, and went along its way. Rav Chiya proceeded to explain that a decree had been pronounced on the traveler, and that the poor man had been sent to give the traveler an opportunity to choose kindness. In so doing, the traveler removed the judgment that was meant to befall him in the form of the first snake. The second snake was sent because the traveler chose to give of his food to the poor man. The two students of Rav Shimon then went to the traveler, shared their food, and told him of his merit to be sent such a gift.

Miracles like this happen to us every day. We are presented with an opportunity just like the traveler, when he was allowed to decide for himself if he was going to give up his last morsels of food and last drop of water. By his own choice, this man was given back his life and became a child of God. If he had known that by giving he would be saved, and he behaved out of his own need, then he would have been a servant of God. The *Zohar* explains that this is why the children of Israel are referred to in these two ways. It is about their choice.

THE GIFT OF RAV ISAAC LURIA (THE ARI)

There is a kabbalistic notion that every person' soul is connected to a righteous soul (*tzadik*). My personal *tzadik* is Rabbi Isaac Luria (the Ari). Every time my next level of growth is in front of me, the Ari illuminates my way. What I have learned from his life and his teachings has benefitted and strengthened me in even the most difficult of tests.

The Ari was born in 1534 CE, in Jerusalem. He was very young when his father passed away, and he and his mother were sent to live with his uncle in Cairo. As a little boy, he was a spiritual prodigy, revealing sacred secrets. When he came of age, the Ari traveled to the banks of the Nile, where he lived alone, spending time studying the *Zohar*, and living in silence. The Ari was able to communicate with all of nature, physical and metaphysical.

At the age of 36, the Ari moved with his wife to the city of Safed, in Israel, where he met his most important student, Chaim Vital. Chaim Vital learned and absorbed the Ari's teachings, eventually compiling them into the text known as the *Writings of the Ari*. These books decode the *Zohar* and organize the secrets of the universe into a system that can be studied, learned, and applied in a practical way to life. Today, we know this system as the Lurianic Kabbalah, and it is the lineage and path we follow in The Kabbalah Centre.

The life of the Ari was short; he left this world at the age of 38. Like many kabbalists, his life was by no means easy. Yet we know that sometimes the more difficult the relationship between a person and his own soul—between a person and the Light—the greater is that person's capacity to draw Light to the world.

For our part, we need to remember that everyone is tested. We are all tested. Sometimes we will pass these tests, and sometimes we will not. But the trick here is to look at the lives of those who came before us and understand that the harder the situation before us, the more spiritual nourishment we can gain from it.

We can connect to the Ari, by studying from his teachings, to strengthen our consciousness and acceptance that our challenges are simply the wrapping around the very gift of Light we seek. However, we cannot receive this Light if we refuse the gift of the tests.

THE LIGHT OF RAV SHIMON BAR YOCHAI

Rav Shimon bar Yochai, the author of the *Zohar*, fled persecution from the Romans. He hid in a cave with his son for 13 years. With little food, they sustained themselves only from the fruit of the carob tree and water from a small spring. To hide, he buried himself in the ground with only his head above the soil. When Rav Shimon emerged from the cave after all those years, he met his father-in-law, Rav Pinchas Ben Yair, who proclaimed, "Oh, that I see you thus!" Rav Shimon's clothes were tattered, and his body was covered in sores. He was withered and frail after living in dirt and barely seeing sunlight for so long. Rav Shimon responded, "If I wasn't as I am, I would not be what I am."

Spirituality is a grinding process. It involves the ability to rise up with each difficulty, from every opportunity, with the understanding that in the midst of it all there is Light, there is growth. It is the way for us to become more.

Rav Shimon's words, "If I wasn't as I am, I would not be what I am," contain a very important lesson for you and me. Without challenges, there is no ladder. Without striving for certainty in the face of difficulties, we cannot reach our goal in our spiritual work—our potential destiny.

It was only after Rav Shimon experienced the severity of the place of his confinement that he was able to manifest his soul's purpose: To reveal the Light and text of the *Zohar*, which came through pain, work, and effort. This is the way of things in our physical world, after all does not life itself—the greatest revelation of Light—come through the labor of the birthing process? Does not the achievement of our purpose come from hard work? There is no birth without the push; there is no satisfaction without hard work.

It is in difficulty that the Light exists, and it is by the contrast of darkness that a candle can shine brightly.

LOVE

Cultivate the Power of an Open Heart

SEE WITH A GOOD EYE

During periods of spiritual growth and tests it can be very tempting to fall into our usual reactive modes of sadness, anger, and perhaps the most destructive, judgment. If we can apply our effort to resist whatever is our tendency, we can tap into higher energies, experience elevated consciousness, and achieve the gift of seeing with a "good eye," as did 18th century Kabbalist, the Baal Shem Tov (Rav Israel ben Eliezer).

When his father died, the great Baal Shem Tov was only a little boy. He was placed into a religious school; he was not treated well by his classmates and did not get along with the head teacher. Futhermore, he had a difficult time with his family. His favorite place to be was in the woods, alone, basking in the beauty amongst the birds and the trees. He loved communing with his Creator in the magnificence of nature.

One day, while in the woods, he met an old man who blessed him with the gift of a "good eye." He was confused by this odd blessing, and not knowing what it meant, shrugged it off and went on his way. When he returned home, he began to notice that everything seemed different. He saw the chaos he had seen before, only now he saw with more than his eyes; he was able to feel with his heart, and that opened his understanding and compassion for why this chaos was taking place.

He saw people who were in pain, reacting to their pain, and by so doing, becoming disconnected from their own Divine essence and the essence of love. He was suddenly aware how, in dealing with their problems, people acted in ways that were disappointing and even hurtful to others. The Baal Shem Tov realized that in a situation that seems negative, there is a cause that led to it, and that cause is exactly the thing for which we need to have empathy.

We have not all had the merit to be blessed with the gift of a "good eye" but we can develop it with some internal discipline. Practically, this means focusing on what is right and good in other people, rather than what is wrong with them. It means looking at people and seeing the beauty of their eyes. It means to have compassion for how hard it is for them to make a living or how difficult it is for them to be with their family. It is easy to see what's wrong with others. To see the good, however, takes effort. To see the good in others is a choice. And if we do not make that choice, then we remain in the world that looks like chaos—chaos not caused by the Divine but by our own selfishness and inhumanity.

Yes, the world is full of negativity. You know why? Because it is humanity's job to change it. It is up to us to be a messenger of love and harmony, rather than hate and intolerance. It is up to us to choose to see others with an eye of kindness. If we can do this, we will have the power to literally lift ourselves out of the realm of judgment and into the realm of love and Light.

OPEN YOUR HEART

Simple gestures, when done with heart, can mean a lot; they can also influence the future beyond what we see in the moment. There is a *Midrash* based on Shemot 3:1 that relates the following:

> *"Moses was shepherding the sheep of Yitro. He saw the burning bush when he went in search of a lost sheep. Moses found the sheep drinking and realized that it had gone looking for water. He took pity on the sheep and carried it back to the flock."*

A shepherd, be it of a flock of sheep or a nation of people, has compassion for his charges. Moses showed such compassion, and God rewarded him with the leadership of the Israelites.

This is a lesson for all of us regarding our spiritual path. Moses was not chosen for his intelligence or for the depth and breadth of his knowledge. What made Moses a leader in the eyes of God was the quality of his heart—his ability to embody the love, care, and harmony that exists within the Creator's Light.

The *Zohar* says:

> *"Come and see, when a man wills himself to worship his Master, the will first reaches the heart,*

which is the basis and foundation of the entire body.
Then that goodwill is diffused in all the members of
the body; and the will of the members of the body
and the will of the heart combine and draw to
themselves the splendor of the Shechinah to rest on
them."

—*Zohar*, Pekudei 5:7

If one has an open heart, then the whole of the individual, and everything around that person, will be affected. The hands, the feet, and even the environment, all react according to the heart's influence.

HEART CHAKRA VISUALIZATION

It is very difficult to live in the world when our heart is closed. And our heart cannot be open if we do not have love for ourselves and for others. To love someone else, it is important to first understand and respect yourself or your love will be conditional. I have included an opening of the heart visualization exercise for you to do when you feel your heart is closing to yourself or to others.

In your mind's eye, see yourself walking on the beach. You feel your soles in the warm sand. You feel a sense of goodness about you, the warmth of the sun, the cool breeze. Just for a few moments sit near the water and watch the ripples. Touch the sand, feel it warming you. As you sit there, imagine how it feels to have the ripples of the sea form a union with your heart; softly and gently feel your heart expanding like the rippling. In this opening, there is self-awareness, there is calm, a joy. You are in a place of contentment, where you feel you are cared for.

Now extend this feeling of love outward. For otherwise, we are half of a being, half of a friend, half of a love—and sometimes we find ourselves to be no being at all. In this exercise, we choose to form a whole being. With the Light that shines out from us with compassion, we find the beauty in our friends and in our loved ones, that at times, we have not looked close enough to find.

Take this Light through your heart, and extend it forward. Now choose someone and send this energy to that person. Share. Share this Light, this joy inside of you. Feel this person light up, through their heart, their head, to their whole being. Feel this person in harmony with you generating a force of unity. And in this energy find forgiveness, if you have hurt each other. Tell this person that you are sorry for the times that you have caused each other pain. Feel the resonance, oneness, warmth, and compassion.

As human beings we are afraid, we stumble and we fall. It is our heart that allows us to see the frailties in each other, and helps us to rise again, walk again, and be friends again. Allow this compassion and warmth to fill you at this moment. Using the letters *Hei-Hei-Ayin* ע·ה·ה, (the 72 Name of God for Unconditional Love) feel the energy run through your being, through the source of life, through the heart, extending out to the person that is with you. Through the Light that streams from *Hei-Hei-Ayin*, generate a love that exists within you without an agenda; without hate; without pain. It is a gift to use these letters. Feel the joy. Take a deep breath through your nose. You are on the beach. It is warm and comfortable. There is a softness as the water hits your feet.

BE THE CONSCIOUSNESS OF LOVE

At this time of great awakening and awareness, the most vital shift that can take place is for humankind to realize that our behavior, and the behavior of the atoms that make up our physical world, are ruled and motivated by a single flow of consciousness. Just as space can come between us and other people in the world, space can also come between the atoms in our bodies. How we interact with each other is reflected in how the atoms of our organs, tissues, and cells interact with one another. Any thought, word, or deed that is in opposition to the Lightforce of Creation simultaneously creates separation on the molecular level.

From this perspective, becoming a sharing, caring, and loving person is not so that we can be good, righteous or live up to an obligation of "I should" do this or that. Rather, becoming a being of true sharing is so that we can align ourselves with the Lightforce of the Creator because when we are in similarity of form with the Force of the Light, we allow Light to become the vibration of our atoms. The Light is always present, and when we attune ourselves to it and act accordingly, all the molecules that make up our being work together harmoniously.

Our vision at The Kabbalah Centre is of a world in which no man will need to teach his neighbor, for all will know the glory of God. In this way, more and more people can become constantly aware of the Divinity that is within and without.

By focusing our hearts and minds on being a force of this love, with God's help, we can sew the fabric of unity that will heal and protect all the countries of the world.

Kabbalah Centre Books

72 Names of God, The: Technology for the Soul
72 Names of God for Kids, The: A Treasury of Timeless Wisdom
72 Names of God Meditation Book, The
And You Shall Choose Life: An Essay on Kabbalah, the Purpose of Life, and Our True Spiritual Work
AstrologiK: Kabbalistic Astrology Guide for Children
Becoming Like God: Kabbalah and Our Ultimate Destiny
Beloved of My Soul: Letters of Our Master and Teacher Rav Yehuda Tzvi Brandwein to His Beloved Student, Kabbalist Rav Berg
Consciousness and the Cosmos (Previously Star Connection)
Days of Connection: A Guide to Kabbalah's Holidays and New Moons
Days of Power Part 1
Days of Power Part 2
Dialing God: Daily Connection Book
Education of a Kabbalist
Energy of the Hebrew Letters, The (Previously Power of the Aleph Beth Volumes 1 & 2)
Fear is Not an Option
Finding the Light Through the Darkness: Inspirational Lessons Rooted in the Bible and the Zohar
Gift of Being Different, The: (Spiritually Hungry Publishing, an imprint of Kabbalah Centre Publishing)
God Wears Lipstick: Kabbalah for Women
Holy Grail, The: A Manifesto on the Zohar
If You Don't Like Your Life, Change It!: Using Kabbalah to Rewrite the Movie of Your Life
Immortality: The Inevitability of Eternal Life
Kabbalah Connection, The: Preparing the Soul for Pesach
Kabbalah for the Layman
Kabbalah Method, The: The Bridge Between Science and the Soul, Physics and Fulfillment, Quantum and the Creator
Kabbalah On The Sabbath: Elevating Our Soul to the Light
Kabbalah: The Power To Change Everything
Kabbalistic Astrology: And the Meaning of Our Lives

Kabbalistic Bible: Genesis
Kabbalistic Bible: Exodus
Kabbalistic Bible: Leviticus
Kabbalistic Bible: Numbers
Kabbalistic Bible: Deuteronomy
Light of Wisdom: On Wisdom, Life, and Eternity
Miracles, Mysteries, and Prayer Volume 1
Miracles, Mysteries, and Prayer Volume 2
Nano: Technology of Mind Over Matter
Navigating The Universe: A Roadmap for Understanding the Cosmic
   Influences that Shape Our Lives (Previously Time Zones)
On World Peace: Two Essays by the Holy Kabbalist Rav Yehuda Ashlag
Origins of Consciousness, The: A Study of the Ten Luminous Emanations
   Volume 1
Path to the Light: Decoding the Bible with Kabbalah: Book of Beresheet
   Volume 1
Path to the Light: Decoding the Bible with Kabbalah: Book of Beresheet
   Volume 2
Path to the Light: Decoding the Bible with Kabbalah: Book of Beresheet
   Volume 3
Path to the Light: Decoding the Bible with Kabbalah: Book of Beresheet
   Volume 4
Path to the Light: Decoding the Bible with Kabbalah: Book of Shemot
   Volume 5
Path to the Light: Decoding the Bible with Kabbalah: Book of Shemot
   Volume 6
Path to the Light: Decoding the Bible with Kabbalah: Book of Vayikra
   Volume 7
Path to the Light: Decoding the Bible with Kabbalah: Book of Bamdibar
   Volume 8
Path to the Light: Decoding the Bible with Kabbalah: Book of Bamidbar
   Volume 9
Prayer of the Kabbalist, The: The 42-Letter Name of God
Power of Kabbalah, The: 13 Principles to Overcome Challenges and
Achieve Fulfillment
Rethink Love: 3 Steps to Being the One, Attracting the One, and
   Becoming One
Rebooting: Defeating Depression with the Power of Kabbalah

Satan: An Autobiography

Secret, The: Unlocking the Source of Joy & Fulfillment

Secrets of the Bible: Teachings from Kabbalistic Masters

Secrets of The Zohar: Stories and Meditations to Awaken the Heart

Simple Light: Wisdom from a Woman's Heart

Shabbat Connections

Tale of the Other Glove, The: (Spiritually Hungry Publishing, an imprint of Kabbalah Centre Publishing)

Taming Chaos: Harnessing the Secret Codes of the Universe to Make Sense of Our Lives

Thought of Creation, The: On the Individual, Humanity, and Their Ultimate Perfection

Tikunei HaZohar: Volumes 1-3

Times of Elevation: Volumes 1-2

To Be Continued: Reincarnation & the Purpose of Our Lives

To the Power of One

True Prosperity: How to Have Everything

Two Unlikely People to Change the World: A Memoir by Karen Berg

Vokabbalahry: Words of Wisdom for Kids to Live By

Way of the Kabbalist, The: A User's Guide To Technology for the Soul

Well of Life: Kabbalistic Wisdom from a Depth of Knowledge

Wheels of the Soul: Kabbalah and Reincarnation

Wisdom of Truth, The: 12 Essays by the Holy Kabbalist Rav Yehuda Ashlag

Zohar, The

The *Zohar*

Composed more than 2,000 years ago, the 23-volume *Zohar* is a commentary on biblical and spiritual matters written in the form of conversations among teachers. It was given to all humankind by the Creator to bring us protection, to connect us with the Creator's Light, and ultimately to fulfill our birthright of transformation. The *Zohar* is an effective tool for achieving our purpose in life.

More than eighty years ago, when The Kabbalah Centre was founded, the *Zohar* had virtually disappeared from the world. Today, all this has changed. Through the editorial efforts of Michael Berg and The Kabbalah Centre, the *Zohar* is available in the original Aramaic language and for the first time in English with commentary.

We teach Kabbalah, not as a scholarly study but as a way of creating a better life and a better world.

WHO WE ARE

The Kabbalah Centre is a non-profit organization that makes the principles of Kabbalah understandable and relevant to everyday life. The Kabbalah Centre teachers provide students with spiritual tools based on kabbalistic principles that students can then apply as they see fit to improve their own lives and by doing so, make the world better. The Centre was founded by Rav Yehuda Ashlag in 1922 and now spans the globe with brick-and-mortar locations in more than 40 cities as well as an extensive online presence. To learn more, visit www.kabbalah.com.

WHAT WE TEACH

There are five core principles:

- **Sharing:** Sharing is the purpose of life and the only way to truly receive fulfillment. When individuals share, they connect to the force of energy that Kabbalah calls the Light—the Infinite Source of Goodness, the Divine Force, the Creator. By sharing, one can overcome ego—the force of negativity.

- **Awareness and Balance of the Ego:** The ego is a voice inside that directs people to be selfish, narrow-minded, limited, addicted, hurtful, irresponsible, negative, angry, and hateful. The ego is a main source of problems because it allows us to believe that others are separate from us. It is the opposite of sharing and humility. The ego also has a positive side, as it motivates one to take action. It is up to each individual to choose whether they act for themselves or whether to also act in the well-being of others. It is important to be aware of one's ego and to balance the positives and negatives.

- **Existence of Spiritual Laws:** There are spiritual laws in the universe that affect people's lives. One of these is the Law of Cause and Effect: What one puts out is what one get back, or what we sow is what we reap.

- **We Are All One:** Every human being has within him- or herself a spark of the Creator that binds each and every person into one totality. This understanding informs us of the spiritual precept that every human being must be treated with dignity at all times, under any circumstances. Individually, everyone is responsible for war and poverty in all parts of the world and individuals can't enjoy true and lasting fulfillment as long as others are suffering.

- **Leaving Our Comfort Zone Can Create Miracles:** Becoming uncomfortable for the sake of helping others taps us into a spiritual dimension that ultimately brings Light and positivity to our lives.

HOW WE TEACH

Courses and Classes. On a daily basis, The Kabbalah Centre focuses on a variety of ways to help students learn the core kabbalistic principles. For example, The Centre develops courses, classes, online lectures, books, and audio products. Online courses and lectures are critical for students located around the world who want to study Kabbalah but don't have access to a Kabbalah Centre in their community. To learn more, visit www.ukabbalah.com.

Spiritual Services and Events. The Centre organizes and hosts a variety of weekly and monthly events and spiritual services where students can participate in lectures, meditation and share meals together. Some events are held through live streaming online. The Centre organizes spiritual retreats and tours to energy sites, which are places that have been closely touched by great kabbalists. For example, tours take place at locations where kabbalists may have studied or been buried, or where ancient texts like the *Zohar* were authored. International events provide students from all over the world with an opportunity to make connections to unique energy available at certain times of the year. At these events, students meet with other students, share experiences and build friendships.

Volunteering. In the spirit of Kabbalah's principles that emphasize sharing, The Centre provides a volunteer program so that students can participate in charitable initiatives, which includes sharing the wisdom of Kabbalah itself through a mentoring program. Every year, hundreds of student volunteers organize projects that benefit their communities such as feeding the homeless, cleaning beaches and visiting hospital patients.

One-on-One. The Kabbalah Centre seeks to ensure that each student is supported in his or her study. Teachers and mentors are part of the educational infrastructure that is available to students 24 hours a day, seven days a week.

Hundreds of teachers are available worldwide for students as well as a study program for their continued development. Study takes place in person, by phone, in study groups, through webinars, and even self-directed study in audio format or online. To learn more visit, www.ukabbalah.com.

Publishing. Each year, The Centre translates and publishes some of the most challenging kabbalistic texts for advanced scholars including the *Zohar*, *Writings of the Ari*, and the *Ten Luminous Emanations with Commentary*. Drawing from these sources The Kabbalah Centre publishes books yearly in more than 30 languages that are tailored for both beginner- and intermediate-level students and distributed around the world.

***Zohar* Project.** The *Zohar*, the primary text of kabbalistic wisdom, is a commentary on biblical and spiritual matters composed and compiled over 2000 years ago and is believed to be a source of Light. Kabbalists believe that when it is brought into areas of darkness and turmoil, the *Zohar* can create change and bring about improvement. The Kabbalah Centre's *Zohar* Project shares the *Zohar* in 30 countries by distributing free copies to organizations and individuals in recognition of their service to the community and to areas where there is danger. Since 2007, over 400,000 copies of the *Zohar* were donated to hospitals, embassies, places of worship, universities, not-for-profit organizations, emergency services, war zones, natural disaster locations, soldiers, pilots, government officials, medical professionals, humanitarian aid workers, and more.

KAREN BERG

KAREN BERG is the Spiritual Director of the Kabbalah Centre. Under her leadership, the Centre has grown from a single location into one of the world's leading sources of spiritual wisdom, with more than 40 locations around the globe. Karen travels extensively to communicate her message of universal spirituality and peace, the very deepest kabbalistic concepts.

She is the founder of Kids Creating Peace, an NGO that offers education programs for personal and societal conflict management and resolution among children and youth in Israel and Palestine. Karen reminds us that the most important way to develop our relationship with God is to see love and goodness in all Gods creation; especially those that are the hardest to love, the people who have hurt us.

Karen's other books include bestselling God Wears Lipstick: Kabbalah for Women, To Be Continued... Reincarnation and the Purpose of Our Lives, and Finding the Light through the Darkness: Inspirational lessons rooted in the Bible and the Zohar. She lives in New York.